# GOD'S PERSONALITY SYSTEM

How the Bible helps
you discover purpose
and direction in life

## Keith Henry

Published by:
How You Work Pty Ltd. P.O.
Box 56 Palm Beach NSW
Australia 2108
howyou.work
keith@howyou.work
Edition 1.2

# Why did we call this book 'God's Personality System'?

God's Personality System comes directly from the Bible and is the clearest description of our personality. It was written over 2,000 years ago with references going back 3,500 years ago. It is referred to in the Bible multiple times and is the most accurate personality description ever because it comes from God, the one who created us and gave us our personality.

For instance, it makes sense to call a person who functions mainly from the heart, a Heart person, same with the Mind person and the Will (strength) person. And last there is the Soul person who is a Big picture person, not into the details.

Jesus answers a question with the words:
*"Love the Lord your God with all your heart and with all your soul, with all your mind and with all your strength (will), and love others as you love yourself". Mark 12:30*

Then, as we look further into the bible, we find our purpose and a list of our Gifts & Talents, with a description of how to use them in our life, relationships and work.

GPS also stands for Global Positioning System which points us in the right direction for our lives.

# CONTENTS

## PART 1

# What is your PURPOSE?

Before we start discovering your purpose, take a moment to answer the following questions:

---

*What am I good at doing but **don't like** doing?*

---

*What am I good at doing, and I **do like** doing?*

---

**How does God see you?**

Discovering your purpose in life all begins with God. So what does the Bible say about how God sees us?

> *"God formed my innermost being shaping my delicate inside and my intricate outside and wove them all together in my mothers womb. I thank you God, for making me mysteriously complex. Everything you do is marvelously breathtaking, it simply amazes me to think about it.. How thoroughly you know me Lord. You even formed every bone in my body when you created me in the secret place, carefully, skillfully shaping me from nothing to something. You saw who you created me to be before I became me. Before I even saw the light of day, the number of days you planned for me were already recorded in your book."*
> **Psalm 139: 3-18 (The Passion)**

> *"For I know the plans I have for you, declares the Lord, plans to prosper you and not to harm you, plans to give you a hope and a future. Then you will call upon me and come and pray to me and I will listen to you. You will seek me and find me when you seek me with all your heart."*
> **Jeremiah 29: 11-14 (NIV)**

> *"God's divine power has already given us everything we need for life and Godliness through our knowledge of Him... by which we have been given to us exceedingly great and precious promises"*
> **2 Peter 1:2-4 (NKJV)**

## God's Personality System

The Bible tells us that each of us is fearfully and wonderfully made, with a unique combination of gifts, talents, and personality traits that make us who we are. Using "God's Personality System" will help you unlock your full potential and find your true purpose in life.

By understanding God's Personality System and how you function best, you can discover your passions, talents, and strengths, and use them to make a positive impact in the world. The Bible tells us to love God with all our **heart, soul, mind,** and strength (**will**), and to love others as ourselves – this is our true selves when we use our gifts and talents to serve others, we are fulfilling our calling and living a life of purpose and meaning.

Don't be afraid to embrace your unique personality traits and use them to pursue your dreams and make a difference in the world. Whether you are a heart person, a mind person, a will (strength) person, or a soul person, God has already given you everything you need to achieve your purpose and fulfil your destiny. Trust in His plan for your life, and use "God's Personality System" to guide you on your journey of self-discovery and personal growth.

Let me ask you a question... *do you know your purpose in life?*

The question of purpose is one that has the power to ignite a deep sense of longing and motivation within us. It's a question that forces us to confront our deepest desires, dreams, and goals. It's a question that has the power to transform our lives in profound and meaningful ways.

If you're someone who feels like you haven't yet found your purpose, know that you're not alone. In fact, many people struggle with this question at some point in their lives. But the truth is that each and every one of us has a unique purpose and mission in life - something that we were put on this earth to do.

When you discover your purpose, it's like a fire ignites within you. You feel a sense of clarity, focus, and direction that propels you forward with purpose and passion. You feel a sense of fulfillment and satisfaction that comes from knowing that you are living out your true calling.

## Why is it so hard to find your PURPOSE?

Aristotle's definition of purpose, he called it happiness... saying that everything and everyone has a purpose or activity for which they are best suited to. We know that a person's purpose and happiness consists in them functioning in the way that they were made. Yet, many people go through their life feeling a little lost, searching for meaning and purpose, why do we go through so much pain, stress and anxiety trying to find our purpose in life?

Maybe, it's because we are not born with the knowledge of who we are, nor is there an instruction manual to show us. We tend to do what our friends, family, school, work or others are doing and what they expect of us. Research shows that it's the same for most people, no matter what their incomes, education, careers, race, or gender; they feel that something is missing from their lives.

## What does SCIENCE say about your PURPOSE?

Professor Brian Cox is the Professor of Particle Physics at the Manchester University and the Royal Society Professor for Public Engagement in Science, UK. He is reported to have an IQ of 183. In his TV show the audience gets to submit questions, and he was asked if the question, "What is the purpose of your life" comes up a lot. He answered, "Yeah, and I always say, if I knew that I would charge more for tickets. Of-course the correct response is that nobody knows, and if anybody tells you they do, they are not worth listening to." [1]

## What do motivational speakers say about your purpose?

After personally coaching more than 50 million people, Tony Robbins has mastered the psychology of success and is considered the world's number one life and business strategist. *"What would life be like if every day you knew with absolute certainty, that you were aligned with your purpose and true self in life... There is one word that will bring you happiness, one: progress. Progress equals happiness. So, if you are asking yourself 'What is my purpose', what you're really asking for is progress, a true sense of fulfilment."*
And then of course Tony goes on to sell tickets to his latest event.

---

[1] *Weekend Australian Magazine, 17th September 2022*

## What do authors and speakers say about finding your Purpose?

Over the years I have read countless books and articles, and watched many videos and presentations. Here's my summary of the common recurring themes.

Finding one's purpose and calling in life can be a challenging and ongoing process that involves self-discovery, exploration, and reflection. While asking questions can be helpful in guiding individuals to explore their goals, motivations, and passions, they may not always lead to clear answers or a definitive sense of purpose.

It is also true that even if a person knows their passions and interests, it may not always be clear what career paths or educational pursuits align with those interests. This is where further exploration and guidance may be necessary, such as career assessments, mentoring, or job shadowing.

Ultimately, discovering one's purpose in life involves a combination of self-reflection, seeking guidance and advice, and trying new things and experiences to learn what resonates with one's values and passions.

**What does the Bible say about Your Purpose?**

God's Personality System comes directly from the Bible and is the clearest description of our personality. It was written over 2,000 years ago with references going back 3,500 years ago. It is referred to in the Bible multiple times and is the most accurate personality description because it comes directly from God, the one who created us and gave us our personality.

*"Love the Lord your God with all your <u>heart</u> and with all your <u>soul</u>, with all your <u>mind</u> and with all your strength (<u>will</u>), and love others as you love yourself".*
**Mark 12:30**

*"For I know the plans I have for you declares the Lord, plans for good and not evil to give you a future and a hope."*
**Jeremiah 29:11**

*"And we know that in all things God works for the good of those who love him, who have been called according to his purpose."*
**Romans 8:28**

*"His divine power has given to us all things that pertain to life and godliness through our knowledge of Him."*
**2 Peter 3**

A more detailed answer is found in Romans 12. In the introduction for the New King James Version of Romans it explains, "Romans teaches us both **theology** and **practice** – how to start and continue a life lived with Jesus"

**Theology:** "The first 11 chapters are a carefully constructed presentation of the gospel of salvation"

**Practice:** "Then embrace chapters 12-16 as you joyfully live-out the life that God has given us"

"We don't all FUNCTION the same" **Romans 12:4**

We have different gifts according to the favour given to us let us use them in proportion to our **faith.** **Romans 12:6**

This word '**faith**' is a translation of the Greek word *pisteōs* which can also be translated *trust* or *confidence.*

The definition of **function** is to operate in the way you are made, so that you can fulfill your purpose. But it's clear from research all over the world that the vast majority of people aren't fulling their purpose. Gallup research found that only 1 in 5 people are productively engaged in their work [1] and the average productivity for office workers is only 3 hours per day.[2]

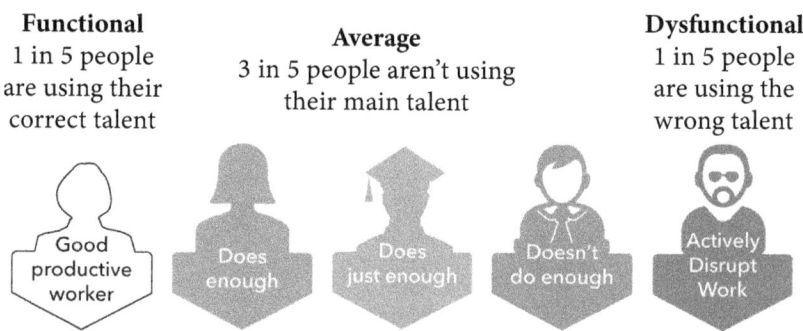

Whether we are talking about a person, or even a tool, you can only function productively by operating in way you were made to work. If you've ever tried to assemble an IKEA flatpack when you're no good with details you'll know this all too well.

### What is your purpose?

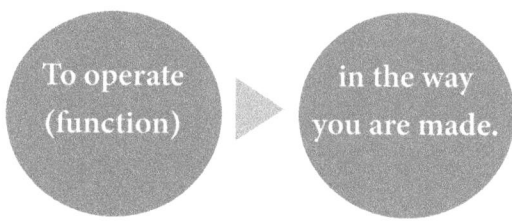

1. Global Employment Enagement *https://www.gallup.com/394373/indicator-employee-engagement.aspx*
2. Office Productivity Survey  *https://www.vouchercloud.com/resources/office-worker-productivity*

"Your purpose is to function in the way you are made by using the gifts you have been given."

- We don't all **function** the same way. (Romans 12:4)

- We all have different **gifts** according to the grace (favour) given to us, let us use it in proportion to our trust. (Romans 12:6)

- It's the perfect will of God for your life. (Romans 12:2)

## The Greek word for Gift is Charisma

Your charisma is your divinely conferred power and talent. It is your compelling attractiveness and charm. Your identity is your name, talent and attraction

1. Your charisma is your **TALENT**. It's the natural ability you are born with to do some things better than anything else you could do; it's your power and your anointing of how you function and operate best so that you can fulfil your purpose. If your talent is 'Encouraging' you would have the natural ability to be able to see what's possible, new opportunities and you would joyfully encourage others

2. Your charisma is your **ATTRACTION**. What makes you attractive? It is your natural charm and attractiveness that others notice and like about you and it's the best way you relate best with other people. For instance, if you are a 'Giver' your natural attraction would be your 'kindness'. Your kindness is what naturally attracts people to you and it's often how you relate with them.

3. Your charisma is your **IDENTITY**. It is the person you are made to be, not only your name; it's also your talent and your attraction. For instance, if your name is Bob and you are a 'Manager', and a builder, you would be identified as Bob the good Builder who is a trustworthy and reliable, who knows all details, how to do the work and will get the job done on time and on budget.

You were born with the talent and ability to do some things well. This also means the opposite is true – there are things you are naturally **not** good at. Unfortunately, most of us learn the hard way that we cannot do everything well.

It is best to know what you are naturally good at and like doing, then develop it and stick to it. We should also be intentional about not doing the things that we aren't naturally good at. Of course there are times in your life when you'll need to complete things that you aren't naturally good at, but you can do this while being more intentional about your long term focus.

As we mentioned before, Gallup research shows that only 1 in 5 people are good and productive in their work. This clearly shows that the majority of people are in the wrong job.

Have a think about the things you are currently doing that you know you aren't naturally good, and if there's a way you can spend less time doing these. Also think about how you can devote more time to doing the things that you are good at.

A school principal in Singapore sent this letter to parents before an exam:

*Dear Parents,*

*The exams for your children are to start soon. I know you are really anxious for your child to do well.*

*But, please do remember, amongst the students who will be sitting for the exams there is an artist, who doesn't need to understand Maths. There is an entrepreneur, who doesn't care about history or English literature. There is a musician, whose Chemistry marks wont matter. There is an athlete whose physical fitness is more important that Physics. If your child does get top marks, that's great. But if he or she doesn't, please don't take away their self-confidence and dignity from them. Tell them it's OK, it's just an exam, they are cut out for much bigger things in life. Tell them, no matter what you score, you love them and will not judge them.*

*Please do this, and when you do, watch your children conquer the world. One exam or a low mark won't take away their dreams and their talent. Please do not think that doctors and engineers are the only happy people in the world.*

Your Notes:

# PART 2

# What is your PERSONALITY?

## Who are YOU?

In this chapter we will ask you questions to discover your personality using God's Personality System from the Bible. Of course everyone is uniquely made and there is no-one else exactly like you. We are looking for your dominant personality attributes where you have more characteristics than others.

## We will ask you questions to find your PERSONALITY?

You will be asked "if you are more this or that". Choose the option that is most dominant, or when you are comparing 3 or more options, start by eliminating the least likely one first. If you are still not sure, read Part 5 about 'Real Stories about Gifted and Talented People' and also Part 6 about 'where you are Naturally Smart'

While most personality programs are good, they often leave people asking for more, such as "What does that mean for me and what should I do now?" We will show you how you can find your purpose and how you can live the life you are made for.

*Jesus answered, "You shall love the Lord your God with all your <u>heart</u>, and with all your <u>soul</u>, and with all your <u>strength</u>, and with all your <u>mind</u>; and your neighbour as yourself."* **(Mark12:30)**

You may have read this scripture many times and not noticed an interesting detail. What Jesus is identifying is there are obvious 'parts' of who we are – our **heart** (the seat of our emotions; the place where we have feelings), our **soul** (the big picture and not the details of the heart, the will and the mind), our **strength** (our **will**, that place where we decide things) and our **mind** (the practical and knowledge people).

We all know heart people, who come at things more through their emotions than through say their mind or their will. And we all know the detailed thinkers, who come at things more through their minds than say through their emotions, and so on. It turns out this is reflected in the "God's Personality System" and is a way of understanding ourselves from a biblical perspective. Ask yourself: "Am I a Heart, Mind, Soul or Will person?"

## Your Personality

Now, it might take a bit of time and reflection to consider each one and think things through. Many, many people have never really thought about these things before and so it mightn't seem quite clear to start with. You may ask your family – do you think this is me? They're often very good observers of us and help us clarify things. But the final choice needs to be yours – it needs to be the one that you identity most with – the one that truly resonates with who you are. So here we go – let's do it.

Now the first one of the four parts of who we are, our four key personalities, is the Soul. At first, I found this the most difficult one of the four to get my mind around. So let me explain. It's pretty straight forward to understand that the human soul is made up of our emotions (our heart, our feelings) and our mind (the place of rational thought where we think and reason) and our will (that part of us where we decide things). And intuitively, we can understand that people could easily approach life more through one of these than the others. So why do we start off with the Soul – the whole of who we are? Because there are some people who approach life rather more holistically than the rest of us. And these are the people whose primary motivation comes out through the soul. The question is – are you one of them?

## Personality in the Bible

Discovering your personality is not a particularly new concept. In fact the Bible, which was written over 6000 years ago, has hints about our unique individual personality. As we have just discussed, Jesus knew that there were different parts to our makeup and these differences play themselves out time after time in our lives.

*Jesus said, "You shall love the Lord your God with all your heart, and with all your soul, and with all your strength (will), and with all your mind; and your neighbour as yourself."*
*(Luke 10:27)*

It turns out that each one of us sees the world more through one of those four, than through the others. So what we're about to do, is to help you to identify your primary personality and your secondary personality.

As you read through the next four parts of this chapter – The Soul, The Heart, The Mind and The Will – chances are that you're going to identify particularly strongly with one of those, more than the other three. You may not agree with everything to do with that particular one, but mostly, it's you. That will be your primary personality. Hang on to that – you're going to need it at the end of this chapter. And there will probably be a second one that partly describes you, but it's not quite you.

Chances are, you'll sense some degree of affinity with it, but you know that the other one (the primary one) is more you than this one. That's the way it's supposed to feel. This second one will be your secondary personality. You'll need that one too.

Let's start by asking you some questions to discover your PERSONALITY

**Are you a WILL or a SOUL or a MIND or a HEART person?**

Now our personality is pretty straightforward to understand. We are made up of our Heart (our emotions, our feelings) and our Mind (the place of rational thought where we think and reason) our Will (that part of us where we decide things) and our Soul (which is a mixture of all 3 but from a big picture point of view, not the details).

Jesus talked about the different parts to our makeup. It turns out that each one of us comes at life more through one of those than the others (our primary personality) and there is a second one that we relate to, but that's not as strong as the first (this is our secondary personality). To make it easy to explain and visualise, "God's Personality System" uses the four quadrants of the clock face to locate those four key personalities. You'll be discovering your primary and secondary personalities.

Because our personalities are different, each of us sees the same thing quite differently. And these differences play themselves out every day at home and at work and when we're out socially. People are seeing things from a different perspective, and so they respond to those things quite differently.

The sad thing is that because most people have never been shown how to understand the different personalities and perspectives of the people around them, they so rarely understand why people react the way they do. We look at someone else, and our default position is that they obviously see things the same way that we do. And when they don't ... well, then it can lead to conflict, misunderstanding and hurts and alienations.

**Objective Thinking** - I am realistic and influenced more by facts and details than by feelings. I find the solution to a problem by using information & logic to find the right answer.

**Subjective Thinking** - I use more sources to make decisions including my experiences, facts, information, and other sources to find multiple solutions to a problem by creatively exploring all the possibilities and choose the best option.

*Tick how many of these words best describe you. Then choose the column that has the most ticks:*

| **Objective** | **Subjective** |
| --- | --- |
| ☐ Logical | ☐ Intuitive |
| ☐ Details | ☐ Feelings |
| ☐ Realistic | ☐ Experiences |
| ☐ Mathematical | ☐ Perspective |
| ☐ Sequential thinking | ☐ Beliefs |
| ☐ Facts | ☐ Imaginative |
| ☐ Organised | ☐ Opinions |
| ☐ Researching | ☐ Instinctive |
| ☐ Practical | ☐ Empathy |
| ☐ Doing | ☐ Personal |
| ☐ Plans & tasks | ☐ Ideas |

On the previous page, choose the column that has the most
ticks and record your answer below.

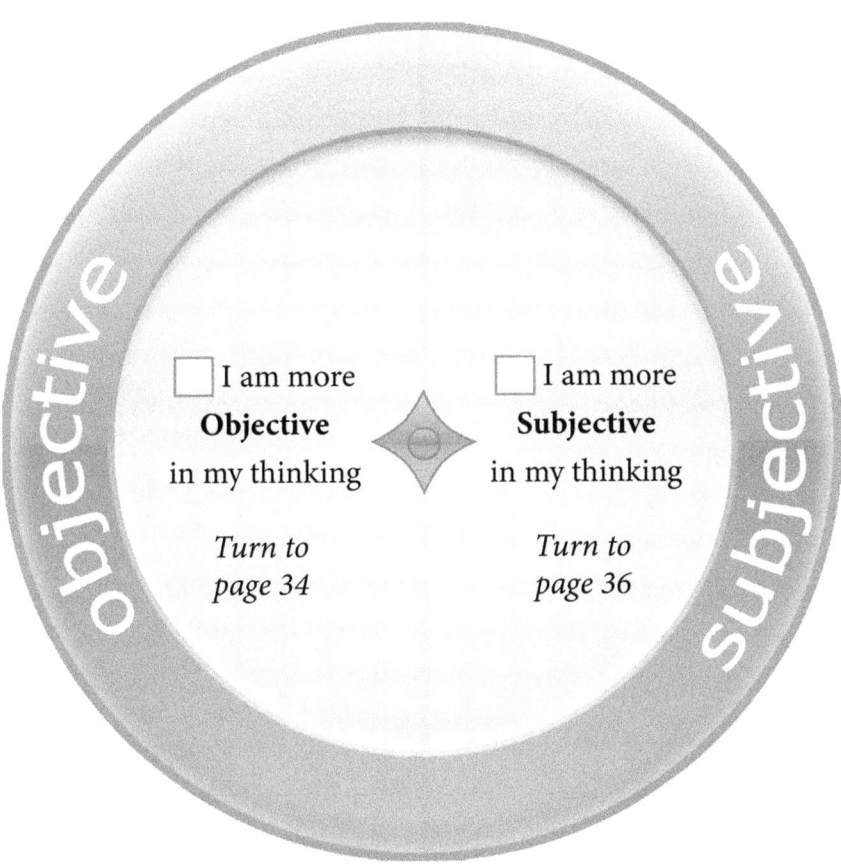

☐ I am more
**Objective**
in my thinking

*Turn to
page 34*

☐ I am more
**Subjective**
in my thinking

*Turn to
page 36*

objective

subjective

We will now discover if you are a Mind or Will person.
*Tick the boxes that best describe you on both of these pages.*

**The Mind Person**

I have a detail-oriented thinking style and prefer to have
all the necessary information before making decisions. I
like to adhere to rules and expectations, and value reading
instructions to ensure I do things correctly. Whether it's hands-
on work or analytical research, I strive for accuracy and take
the time needed to achieve it. My preference for structure and
planning make me a reliable member of a team or project, and
my thoroughness helps ensure successful outcomes. While
my approach may take more time, my commitment to getting
things right is a valuable asset.

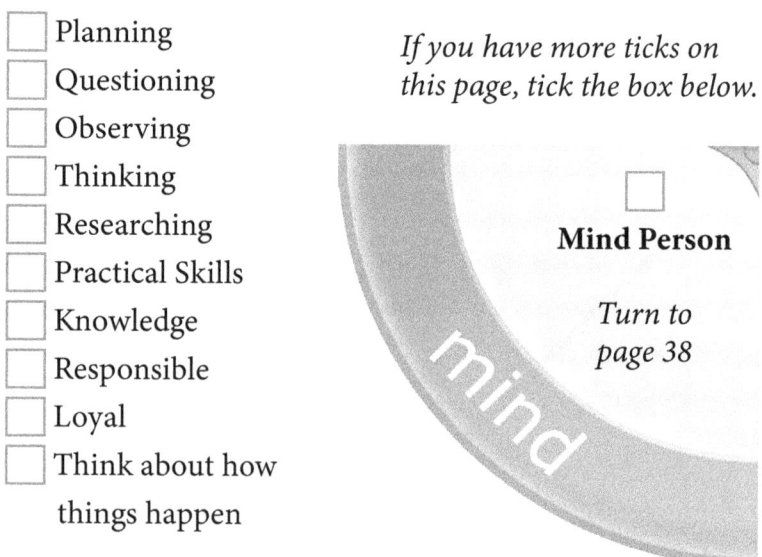

☐ Planning
☐ Questioning
☐ Observing
☐ Thinking
☐ Researching
☐ Practical Skills
☐ Knowledge
☐ Responsible
☐ Loyal
☐ Think about how
   things happen

*If you have more ticks on
this page, tick the box below.*

☐

**Mind Person**

*Turn to
page 38*

**The Will Person**

I am naturally organized and practical in my approach to life. I like to have a clear understanding of the situation at hand before making decisions, and I strive to be realistic in my expectations. I enjoy problem-solving and using logical reasoning to make decision. I like doing the right thing, being punctual, and fulfilling my commitments. I am a natural leader and enjoy managing projects, and motivating other. I have a strong drive and a lot of energy, which I put into everything I do. My strengths lie in my logical thinking, ability to manage, lead, and my competitive nature.

- [ ] Purposeful
- [ ] Decisive
- [ ] Problem Solving
- [ ] Facts
- [ ] Challenging
- [ ] Leading
- [ ] Managing
- [ ] Integrity
- [ ] Organised

*If you have more ticks on this page, tick the box below.*

Will

- [ ] **Will Person**

*Turn to page 38*

We will now discover if you are a Soul or Heart person.
*Tick the boxes that best describe you on both of these pages.*

## The Soul Person

I bring a unique perspective to any situation. Instead of getting bogged down in the details, I focus on the big picture and see possibilities and options that others might miss. This allows me to create by connecting the dots, to communicate new ideas and support people by showing and teaching them. With a passion for good design and a natural talent for innovation, I like to achieve my goals and succeed in what I do. But what really sets me apart is my positive and encouraging nature. I love being around other people and thrive in social settings where I can inspire and motivate those around me.

☐ Passionate
☐ Motivational
☐ Encouraging
☐ Entrepreneurial
☐ Teaching
☐ Leading
☐ Opportunities
☐ Communicator

*If you have more ticks on this page, tick the box below.*

☐

**Soul Person**

*Turn to page 38*

## The Heart Person

I am driven by my emotions. I place a high value on all of my relationships, whether they be with friends, family, or colleagues in both school and work settings. People are the cornerstone of my life, and I take great joy in caring for and helping them. One of my greatest strengths is my ability to sense the emotions and needs of others. Using this, I am able to provide support and understanding to those who are hurting or in need. While I can sometimes be overly sensitive to my own emotions, I find that when I use my gifts to benefit others, they are greatly blessed by my empathy and insight.

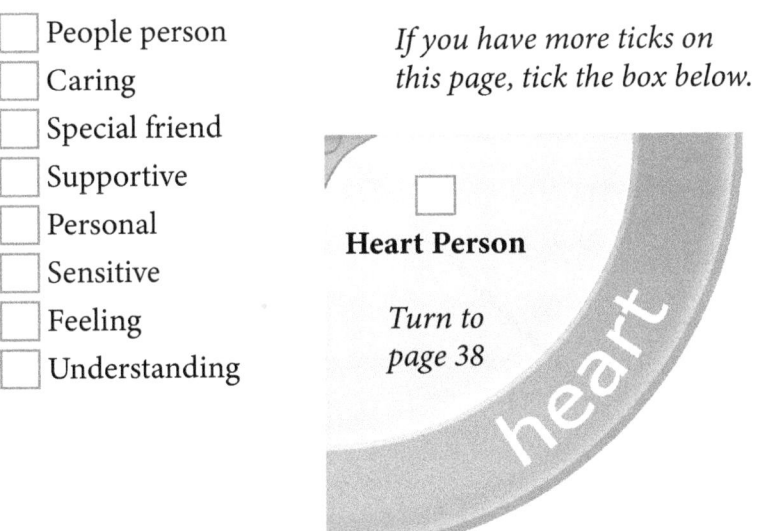

- People person
- Caring
- Special friend
- Supportive
- Personal
- Sensitive
- Feeling
- Understanding

*If you have more ticks on this page, tick the box below.*

**Heart Person**

*Turn to page 38*

heart

## Your Second Personality preference

Now that you've discovered your main personality, let's think about your second preference. Which of these would you say you relate to as well? *Write a '2' in that box.*

☐ As a **SOUL** person, I am more holistic and like to see the big picture, whereas other personalities specialise more in the tasks and details. By viewing things this way I see new concepts, new opportunities and ideas, which enables me to create, to communicate, to teach and support projects. Good design is also important to me. I am a positive person who likes to be innovative and achieve my goals to succeed. I like being around other people, to socialise and mix with them.

☐ As a **HEART** person I am a feelings person. I value my relationships with friends, family and work colleagues. People are the most important part of my life and I like to care for them and help them. I have a natural ability to sense people's feelings and to understand their hurts and needs. I sometimes can be too sensitive to my own feelings, but when I use my sensitivity for others, they are really invigorated by my intuition and understanding of them.

☐ As a **MIND** person, I am into the details. I like to research and get all the facts, taking more time to make decisions. I like to know the rules and to read the instructions. I am either a practical hands-on person or am more academic. I like to be organised and I appreciate a neat and tidy environment. I like being part of a group or team . Being naturally loyal to my groups, they know they can rely on me and I am willing to work hard behind the scene to support them.

☐ As a **WILL** personal, I am logical and realistic. I prefer to make decisions based on judgements, facts and knowledge. I can make quick and firm decisions to put into action. I am good at doing projects, leading teams, managing and giving advice. I am quite competitive especially in sports, games, debating, etc... I like to win and have a lot of drive and energy to put into life. I am good at maths and I like problem solving. I am also decisive, logical, practical and realistic.

# The SOUL Personality

It's pretty straight forward to understand that the human soul is made up of our heart (our emotions, our feelings) and our mind (the place of rational thought where we think and reason) and our will (that part of us where we decide things) and our soul (which is a mixture of all 3 but from a big picture point of view, not the details. People approach life more through one of these than the others. Some people approach life rather more holistically ... whose primary personality comes out through the soul, does this describe you?

You are holistic – meaning that you like to look at the Big picture, not the details.

- You are good at thinking up with new ideas.
- You are innovative and enthusiastic.
- You like to make plans for the future.
- You are open minded and flexible.
- You are positive and idealistic.
- You are talkative and like enjoying life.
- You like spending time with friends and family.
- You are a people person.

## Who are the SOUL people?

People who approach life holistically tend to be big-picture thinkers who are able to see the connections and relationships between different things. They tend to be creative and innovative, often coming up with new ideas and solutions to problems. They are also enthusiastic about life and tend to have a positive, idealistic outlook.

They are good at making plans for the future and are open-minded and flexible in their approach. They enjoy spending time with friends and family and are often described as being talkative and outgoing. They are also known for being people-oriented and enjoy building strong relationships with others. Overall, people who approach life holistically tend to have a positive and optimistic outlook on life and are able to see the bigger picture beyond the details.

The soul people are more inclined to approach life through a holistic lens, meaning that they prioritize the bigger picture and inter-connectedness of things rather than focusing on details. They can draw a little on another side for example their emotional and intuitive side or their analytical and rational side to make decisions and navigate life depending on what their 2nd supportive personality is. Others may be more inclined to approach life through a specific aspect of the soul, such as the heart or mind. For example, someone who is more heart-centred may prioritize their emotions and feelings in decision-making, while someone who is more mind-centred may prioritise logic and reason.

## Why we need SOUL people?

They're the people, people – some of them, the extroverts, are the life of the party. And they're the ones who are happy to break the mould, think outside the square and take us to new places that we may never have gone to without them.

Now imagine we're a family – the four of us, mum, dad and two kids – and we're about to go on a holiday. We have to get from one city to the next, and it's going to be a very long, twelve hour drive. The soul person among us is easy to pick. He or she is the one who wants to stop along the way. It's a hot day, and we drive past a swimming pool. Let's stop and go for a swim! Let's stop for an ice cream. Oh look – a zoo. Why don't we stop and have a look? That'd be great fun! And if we don't get there today – that's fine. We can stop somewhere overnight. We can get there tomorrow. But along the way – let's stop and have some fun?

At workshops we, in effect, do what you're doing right now – we work out what is your primary personality. And once we've done that, we arrange everyone on four separate tables – one for the Soul, one for the Heart, one for the Mind and one for the Will. It is amazing to observe how the 4 different personalities behave, they are so different from each other. And for the rest of the workshop – you can see the Soul people laugh and carrying on having an outrageous amount of fun, so it seems. They don't always quite finish everything, but hey, they have lots of fun along the way

# The HEART Personality

The Heart people are sensitive to people's feelings and to people's needs. They naturally get beside people to help them and you can find them in all care  industries such as nursing, aged care, community care, welfare, foodcare, etc. Some also have an amazing artistic flair and are good at design, acting, art, fashion design, interior design, etc. The Carer loves caring and the Giver loves helping people. Are you one of them? Does This Describe You?

• You look for personal meaning when making decisions – how will it affect other people?

• You're good at listening and you're sensitive to how other people feel.

• You like spending time with people.

• You tend to appreciate creativity, music or art.

• You like helping people that you care about

• You are sensitive to people's needs.

• You are supportive of others.

• You are a carer or a giver

## Who are the HEART people?

The question is – which one of us is the heart person? Well that's easy – you can pick the heart person a mile off. They are the one who makes sure we have some drinks in the car with us, and some fruit to eat, a packet of lollies and some chips.

Oh, and a box of tissues – mustn't forget the tissues. And then they put them all at their feet on the passenger's side. Now our kids have grown up and so there's no one in the back seat anymore these days, but she has to have all these things at her feet, making her uncomfortable because she can't stretch out. Why? Because someone might need something of course! Isn't it obvious?

It may be that you or I are motivated primarily by a part of us other than our hearts. But when we are broken hearted – we need someone who can reach our heart, don't we? We need someone who can feel with us, hurt with us, cry with us and touch our emotions and touch our heart in a healing way. And it doesn't have to be some devastating, cataclysmic situation which tears our hearts apart either. Just in the rough and tumble of the day, our hearts can be bruised – our emotions hurt. Whatever it is, however big or small, when our heart aches, right at that moment, we need someone who knows how to speak our heart-language, because that's the part of us that needs speaking to. And so it's pretty much self-evident why Carers are motivated first and foremost through their emotions and their heart.

When our heart aches, we don't need an Achiever to inspire us on to greater achievements. We don't so much need an Encourager to make us feel good either. Nor do we need a Teacher right at that point. What we need right at that moment is the Carer – someone who can care for us. The Carer is moved by their heart because they have a deep sense of empathy and compassion towards others. They prioritize the emotional needs of those around them and are driven by a desire to alleviate any pain or suffering they may be experiencing. The Carer is a beautiful embodiment of empathy and compassion, with a heart overflowing with love for others. Their unwavering dedication to meeting the emotional and physical needs of those around them is nothing short of inspiring.

Their nurturing and caring nature makes them attentive to the needs of others and they are always ready to provide comfort and support when needed. Their nurturing nature creates a safe space for those in need, where they can find comfort, support, and healing. The Carer knows that sometimes it's the small acts of kindness, a gentle word or a warm embrace, that can make the biggest difference in someone's life.

The Carer understands that sometimes words are not enough, and that actions speak louder than words. They know that a simple gesture of kindness, such as offering a tissue or a snack, can make a big difference in someone's day. Their commitment to being a constant source of love and support, no matter how difficult the circumstances may be, is truly remarkable. The Carer understands that the road to healing can be long and challenging, but their love for others is stronger than any obstacle.

Overall, the Carer's motivation through the heart is a powerful force that drives them to make a positive impact in the lives of those around them. the Carer's motivation through the heart is a beacon of hope and a shining example of what it means to truly care for others.

**Why we need HEART people?**

Well, frankly, these are the people who care for us. They're the ones who are prepared and able to meet our emotional and physical needs. Imagine again that we're a family of four, preparing for the long, twelve hour car drive. We already know who the soul person is in our midst. They're planning what fun we're going to have along the way. The question is – which one of us is the heart person? Well that's easy – you can pick the heart person a mile off. My wife's one of them. She's the one who makes sure we have some drinks in the car with us, and some fruit to eat, a packet of lollies and some chips. Oh, and a box of tissues – mustn't forget the tissues. And then ... then she puts them all at her feet on the passenger's side. Now our kids have grown up and so there's no one in the back seat anymore these days, but she has to have all these things at her feet, making her uncomfortable because she can't stretch out. Why? Because someone might need something of course! Isn't it obvious? Not to me, but it is to the heart people. And that's why we need these people – the heart people – because they care for us.

It's true, the heart people are often the ones who make sure everyone's needs are met, and they do it out of a genuine desire to care for others. They are the ones who remember birthdays and anniversaries, and they are always there with a shoulder to cry on. They may not always be the most rational or logical, but they make up for it with their empathy and compassion. In a family, they are often the glue that holds everyone together. And in society as a whole, we need heart people to remind us of our humanity and to take care of those who may be overlooked or forgotten.

## The MIND Personality

We all have a mind. We all think about things. But some people experience the world predominantly through their minds. They think things through to a 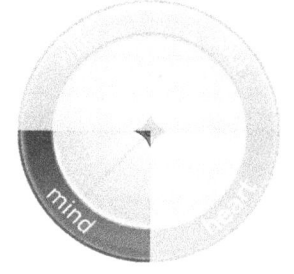 level of detail that seems utterly extraordinary to the rest of us. They're the ones who often become the experts in their field.

Because they are naturally detail people they are the ones that develop the skills to do a task better than anyone else. Many develop a technical skillset such as in trades, gardens, etc while others become knowledgeable and recognised for their expertise and abilities. Their skills can come in many areas such as programming, coding, cooking, police, defence, teaching, etc.

These individuals have an incredible ability to analyse, process and understand complex information with ease. They have a keen eye for detail and a remarkable capacity for critical thinking. They develop a technical skills set that makes them stand out from the rest. They're the ones who become the experts in their field, mastering their craft with precision and finesse.

## Who are the MIND people?

The passage explores the idea that as the world becomes more advanced and sophisticated, things tend to become more complex. It highlights the example of the financial market, where in the past, most people had a simple savings account, but now, many people are involved in the stock market, superannuation schemes, and even financial futures and derivatives trading. This requires a lot of detailed knowledge and expertise to navigate successfully.

An example of designing and laying out a garden. It's not just about making it look pretty, but also ensuring it meets practical needs, puts the right plants in the right places, and connects the spaces while maintaining distinct "rooms". Achieving all of these elements requires a lot of detailed planning, knowledge, and experience. In such complex scenarios, detailed thinkers are the ones who can own the detail with a passion. They are the ones who can analyse, plan, and execute tasks with precision and attention to detail, which are essential for success.

Moreover, the importance of having these detailed thinkers around us is that they help us navigate complex situations, plan ahead, and make informed decisions. They provide a sense of security and stability, particularly in scenarios like a long car trip or a caravan journey where careful planning and execution can make a significant difference. You are planned and organised. You like to spend time researching and getting all the details before making decisions. Because you like to be planned and structured, decision-making takes you more time. You put off decision-making until you have all the details. You notice the dangers and the pitfalls. You are loyal and responsible, You don't like too many demands at the one time, You get anxious and tend to be a worrier when under stress.

## Why we need MIND people

As much as we'd like to think sometimes that life is simple, it isn't. Things can be very complex – the more an economy develops, the more knowledge the human race acquires, the more complex things become. Look at the financial markets. When I was a kid, we all had a passbook account with the bank, and we received annual interest. These days, many, many people own shares on the stock market. They run their own superannuation schemes, not to mention financial futures and derivatives trading. Or something as apparently simple as designing and laying out a garden so that it not only looks nice, but it also connects the spaces while maintaining distinct "rooms", it meets our practical needs, it puts the right plants in the right places ... even that takes a lot of detailed knowledge.

So, there are plenty of things in this world that are complex. And the mind people – they're the ones who will own the detail with a passion. And the rest of us, we definitely need these detailed thinkers around us. Now let's go back again to our family's 12 hour car trip. Again, the mind people are easy to pick out from the crowd. They're the ones who plan ahead – it's going to take 12 hours, we'll take this road, we can stop for breakfast after two hours at this petrol station – but only for a short time. Our main lunch break will be around 12:15 – by then we'll have travelled this far ... and we'll only have this much more to go. We can fill up the tank then and ... that puts us at our destination between 4:45 and 5:00 pm, presuming that we don't run into any delays.

# The WILL Personality

Some people are just driven. Doesn't matter what obstacle lies in the way, they're "programmed" to crash through it or go around it or go over the top of it – whatever it takes. These are people who overcome obstacles by exercising the strength of their will. Sometimes, we find them quite bruising, and we're likely to tell them – "Have a heart! Don't you feel for that person? Stop and have some fun." Nevertheless, they have a strength that the rest of us need.

The question is – are you one of them? Does this describe you?

• You are practical, logical and realistic, good at problem solving and maths
• You prefer to make decisions based on facts, criteria and knowledge.
• You make quick and firm decisions that you put into action.
• You are naturally competitive.
• You are disciplined and punctual and organised
• You are a doer rather than a watcher.
• You like to get to the point and get the facts
• You are active and adventurous.

# Who are the WILL people?

A strong-willed person is someone who possesses a high level of determination, persistence, and perseverance in achieving their goals or objectives, even in the face of obstacles or setbacks. This type of person is often self-motivated and driven, and is willing to put in the effort and hard work necessary to succeed.

Some common traits of a strong-willed person include:

## 1.Determination
A strong-willed person is highly motivated to achieve their goals and is willing to work hard to accomplish them.

## 2.Persistence
This type of person is not easily discouraged by setbacks or failures, and will continue to work towards their goals even when faced with challenges.

## 3.Resilience
A strong-willed person is able to bounce back from setbacks and failures, and is able to learn from these experiences in order to improve their performance in the future.

## 4.Self-discipline
This type of person has the ability to control their impulses and to stick to a plan or schedule in order to achieve their goal

**5.Confidence**

A strong-willed person has a strong sense of self-confidence and belief in their abilities, which helps them to overcome challenges and achieve success.

Overall, a strong-willed person is someone who is highly motivated, persistent, and determined in achieving their goals. They possess a unique combination of traits and characteristics that enable them to stay focused, work hard, and overcome obstacles in order to achieve their objectives.

**Why we need WILL people?**

Well, we need them – because these are the people who get things done. strong leaders and managers are critical to the success of any organization. They provide direction, motivation, decision- making, and resource management skills that are essential for achieving a persons or organization's goals and objectives.

- Do you want a project started, planned, organised and completed?
- Do you have an idea but you can't quite make the rubber hit the road?
- Is there some obstacle blocking your path?
- Well, grab one of these will people, get them on your side, and they'll make it happen for you.

Now, you can pick them on the twelve hour car trip without any problem. They're the ones that make the whole family pack everything up the night before and put it down at the front door, so they can pack the car quickly and efficiently in the morning. Then, they want you up no later 3:30 am (not a minute later!) and in the car by 4:00 am for an on-time departure. And then they just drive and drive and drive. Because the trip, after all, is all about getting there. "Dad, I need to go to the toilet" one of the children remonstrates from the back seat after two hours and forty-one minutes of driving (a long time, after all, for a child). Dad looks at his watch. "Well, in another hour or so, we'll be stopping for a quick five minutes to get some petrol. You can hang on 'til then." God love 'em – but they do get things done. They get us to where we want to go.

## PART 3

# Discover your gifts and talents

## Having Different Gifts

Let's take a look at Romans 12:6 (NIV)

*We have different gifts, according to the grace given to each of us. If your gift is prophesying, then prophesy in accordance with your faith; if it is serving, then serve; if it is teaching, then teach; if it is to encourage, then give encouragement; if it is giving, then give generously; if it is to lead, do it diligently; if it is to show mercy, do it cheerfully.*

These gifts are sometimes referred to as the motivational gifts, but we like to call them **God's Personality System**. In other words, the DNA of who God made us to be. God's Personality System is a program which comes from the heart of God.

God's heart is for all of us to know our identity, who we are and to know that we are purposely designed for great purposes. 'GPS' opens the door for greater understanding and even revelation for us to know our qualities and our uniqueness. With this breakthrough program you will very quickly grow in confidence.

Being in agreement with your design and purpose allows you to boldly move forward in the journey of life. This allows us to step out on a strong foundation of acceptance and understanding where better choices produce better results and successful living. Through GPS we can all fulfil more of our potential.

## Your Gifts and Talents are essential to finding your purpose

Every person is born with a unique set of talents that gives them a special ability to perform certain kinds of tasks easily and much better than anything else they could do. Yet. It also make other tasks seem hard. Knowing what you do best– what your strongest natural abilities are and how you are "hard-wired", then finding how it best fits into your work and life and are fundamental to finding your purpose and fulfilment.

Peter Drucker, who Fortune magazine described as the most visionary business coach of his time, said, "Most people think they know what they are good at, they are usually wrong." Gallup Research found only 1 in 5 people are properly engaged in their work, meaning most people could be in the wrong job. It's not how qualified or experienced a person is, if they don't have the right talent for the task, they are unlikely to be productive

## Why is it important to know your talents?

Your talent is your natural ability that determines the ease or difficulty that you experience in doing certain types of activities. When a particular task requires a set of abilities that are natural for you, you can perform it in less time, with less effort, and with more passion and enjoyment.

On the other hand, when a task requires talents that are not in your natural make up, you spend more time, more effort, and exert more energy than is usual to achieve an average to poor level of performance. People can only work for short periods of time, usually 20 minutes before they need to take a break.

That explains why certain activities are relatively easy for one person, but hard for another.

Take a moment to think about the things that are easy for you to do, that others find difficult. You might want to write them in the space below.

## Your Attraction is essential to finding your purpose

One of the most important, the most profound, the most fundamental influence on our lives is how we see ourselves. And let me say, how we see ourselves, isn't always that healthy. So. what sort of an impact is that having on your life?

Then, there is the other side, how do others see us? What about the impact that we have on the lives of other people. Work, home, family, friends, relatives, school and work colleagues, the life that we live out, day after day after day. In the morning when we get up, during the day at work or at school or at home, whatever it is we do, in the evening when we come home again at dinner time. Just the accumulation of little things that we do every day the simple things, the nice things we say, the not so nice things we say, the encouragement we give to people, the criticism we meet out sometimes. 2000 years ago the apostle Paul wrote a letter to a church in Galatia and he talks about the two different sides of who we are. Bible teacher Berni Dymet paraphrases Paul's letter:

*"Look, you have a human nature and our nature being what it is, we can be selfish and grumpy and we can do all that stuff and we can actually bear some bad fruit in our lives. On the other side we have a capacity to have a relationship with God and out of that relationship, we can have good relationships with other people"*

**How do we relate with our family, friends and colleagues?**

Animals can sometimes teach us a lot about good relationship Dale Carnegie's book titled *How To Win Friends and Influence People* says 'Our best role models might not be people at all. Perhaps dogs are better. "Dogs are man's best friend for a reason. When we return home, dogs welcome us as heroes. They never demean us or mock us. They exist to befriend us. Are they ever without pure joy just being in our presence?" And the nursery rhyme 'Mary had a little lamb' tells us why the lamb loves Mary. "Why does the lamb love Mary so? Why, because Mary loves the lamb you know"

Maybe we can all share a bit of love around when we focus on blessing others and not ourselves.

**Your Identity is essential to finding your purpose**

Without our identity intact, without a deep knowledge of who we are, who God made us to be – how can we possibly head off down the path that He ordained for us before time began? Should I become a doctor or a builder? Should I aspire to being a leader, or am I more the type to be a researcher in a university? Should I write a book, or find someone who can write it with me? Should I ... ?

All those depend on knowing who we are! So how could we not want to know who we are? When we talk about being the person we were made to be, the first part of that is knowing that God made us the way we are. I'm not supposed to be like the next person. I'm not supposed to have your gifts and your talents, or the looks of that person over there or anyone else. I'm supposed to be me. I'm supposed to be who God made me to be. And the same with you. You're supposed to be who God made you to be. Each person has different talents, desires, different strengths and different limitations.

And secondly our lives aren't about some karma or vague sense of chance or destiny. Our lives have a definite plan. Before any of the days yet existed, every day was ordained for you and for me and was written in God's book, God's blueprint. Our DNA and our days. Who we are and what would happen; the years ahead, every thought, every desire, every dream, every hope, every hurt, every experience. He knit us together in our innermost being and set every day before us according to His plan.

You and I are who we are because that's how He made us. Even if we've gone off the rails – that's no surprise to Him. Even if we've wandered completely away from His ideal for our lives, He's gently calling us back. God's not having a panic attack at this very moment, because instead of doing what He prepared for us, we've wandered off and done completely the opposite.

He can cope with that, that's what grace is all about. And knowing this stuff is profound and wonderful and beautiful! Tragically, so many people spend much of their lives not liking themselves when they have not ever found out who God made them to be. It's hard to be the amazing person God made you to be if you don't know who you are and you are not living it. Let me challenge you today. Let me get right in your face with this...

## Are you prepared to start living every day as the person God made you to be?

*Having different GIFTS according to the grace (favour)
God has given us, let us use them... in proportion to our
trust. - Romans 12:6*

We will now discover your main talent. We will give you
a brief summary of each talent, followed by more detailed
information. Take your time to find the talent that is most like
you. Sometimes it can be helpful to exclude the talents that
aren't like you.

Previously we found out if you were a Soul, Heart, Mind or
Will person (refer to pages 34-37)

If you are a **Will** person, turn to page 73.

If you are a **Soul** person, start on the next page.

If you are a **Mind** person, turn to page 68.

If you are a **Heart** person, turn to page 65.

will soul mind heart

*Choose which of these best describe you. Over this page and the next, tick the boxes that are most like you. Then choose the box that has the most ticks.*

I am like an architect or marketer who can see the Big Picture and can see where everyone and everything fits best & how to get the best results from people & projects.

☐ Goal Focused
☐ Likes to be active
☐ Productive
☐ Team player/leader
☐ Competitive
☐ Motivated to succeed
☐ Has a to-do list

*If you have more ticks above, tick the box below.*

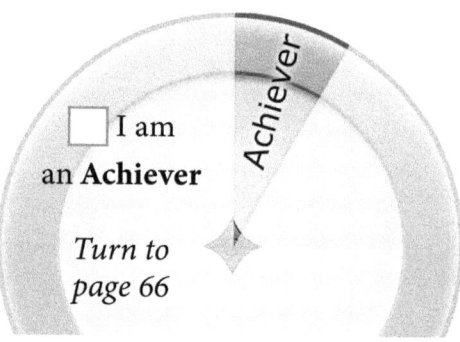

☐ I am
an **Achiever**

Achiever

*Turn to page 66*

I can see the Big Picture and the positive side of life. I see potential and future possibilities and I have lots of options and new ideas but like to avoid the nitty-gritty details

- [ ] Enthusiastic
- [ ] Good communicator
- [ ] Social
- [ ] Likes variety
- [ ] Bored with routine
- [ ] Entrepreneurial
- [ ] Creative

*If you have more ticks above, tick the box below.*

- [ ] I am an **Encourager**

Encourager

*Turn to page 67*

I am inclusive of people and receptive to new ideas and programs. I am holistic and can bring people and programs together by engaging and teaching people.

- [ ] Friendly
- [ ] Good listener
- [ ] Stable
- [ ] Teaching
- [ ] Inclusive
- [ ] Relational
- [ ] Diplomatic

*If you have more ticks above, tick the box below.*

- [ ] I am a **Mentor**

Mentor

*Turn to page 68*

# The Achiever

**MY TALENT**: You are like an architect in that you have a natural ability to see where everyone and everything fits, what needs to be done and to organise and allocate the tasks and resources to achieve it. You are good at leading a team and motivating and training them to achieve their goals and be successful. You are a busy person as you get satisfaction by achieving tasks and projects. You are the big picture WILL person of the SOUL and you are productive, persistent and passionate.

**MY ATTRACTION**: You have a passion for life and don't limit yourself as some others might as you want to be successful. Yet you also have patience with people, knowing that all you have to do is to position, train and motivate them to be successful. Many people like to be around successful people who have a positive passion for life and a can-do attitude and who inspire others to be successful.

**MY IDENTITY**: Your identity is the Achiever. There are people who make things happen, and there are people who watch things happen and there are people who wonder what happened. To achieve and be successful you need to be the person who makes things happen.

**MY PURPOSE**: Your purpose is to achieve and motivate others to achieve. Firstly, you are the driver, not a passenger, as Achievers like to make things happen. We can rely on you to set goals and to tick each one off to get things done. Secondly, you motivate the rest of us to get things done and you inspire us and bring out the best in us. And as an Achiever you are competitive and like to win, to be first and to succeed in everything that you do.

# The Encourager

**MY TALENT:** You have a creative ability to communicate information and ideas to others and a natural gift for encouraging, persuading and motivating people. You have the talent to see outside-the-box options by connecting the dots together between seemingly unrelated information and can put them together to create a new idea, product, opportunity or innovation. You are the big picture Mind person of the Soul.

**MY ATTRACTION:** You relate by encouraging others, you boost their self-esteem, enhance their self- confidence, motivate them, lift their spirits and inspire them to be successful in their activities. You bring fun, enjoyment and encouragement from your heart and it's always available. Be encouraging but do also learn to never be critical.

**MY IDENTITY:** Your identity is to be the ENCOURAGER. This means you bring joy, fun and happiness to others by your positive and enthusiastic personality.

**MY PURPOSE:** Your purpose is to Encourage others. If people don't have an Encourager in their life right now, then find one, and they'll be amazed at how encouragers make you feel. The word encouragement comes from the French word, meaning to give heart to. And that's what our Encouragers do, they lift us up, they brighten our day and help us to feel good.

# ■The Mentor

**MY TALENT:** You have a talent to mentor and support others and to facilitate tasks through your friendly and easy going nature. You have the ability to listen attentively and ask questions. You easily accept and include others and you are open minded to differences and do not criticise people. You easily empathise with others and are sensitive to their feelings. You are the big picture Heart person of the Soul.

**MY ATTRACTION:** Your attraction is that you are a calm, peaceful, friendly and happy person, who does not judge or criticise. People like you because you relate by including everyone equally and welcome them. People feel comfortable and relaxed in your presence. You are a good friend who always keeps in touch with your family and friends.

**MY IDENTITY:** You are the mentor-teacher, a facilitator which means you support others and have a way of making life more pleasant and happy for many people through your friendly connection with them.

**MY PURPOSE:** Because of your calm, supportive nature you make a natural supporter and a good facilitator by teaching/ training, mentoring and supporting others. You are a good at listening and identify easily with friends and colleagues. Your friendly, sociable nature means you would make a good teacher and any thing to do with relationships. You are also very diplomatic.

I have a heart of compassion & can sense when people are hurting. I make decisions based on how it affects others. Sometimes I can get caught up in the up and downs of my emotions.

☐ Empathy
☐ Compassion
☐ Intuition
☐ Expression
☐ Artistic
☐ Design

I am sensitive to people's needs, especially those who need help. I am generous with my time, often putting my own needs aside. My gift is getting beside people to help and support them.

☐ Helping
☐ Listening
☐ Generous
☐ Giving
☐ Supportive
☐ Sensing

*If you have more ticks above, tick the box below.*

☐ I am
a **Carer**

*Turn to
page 70*

Carer

*If you have more ticks above, tick the box below.*

☐ I am
a **Giver**

*Turn to
page 71*

Giver

**MY TALENT:** You have a heart of compassion for people, especially for those who are hurting. You relate to people based upon your emotions and you like to understand what others are feeling. You also tend to make your judgements and decisions based more by your feelings of how it affects people than facts and figures. Your feelings and imagination can also empower your artistic and your acting abilities.

**MY ATTRACTION:** When you spend time with people you speak as a warm and caring person. You like to relate with friends with a cuddle, and you are expressive with your feelings. You can also express yourself in artistic and creative ways. Most people appreciate the way you care and understand them.

**MY IDENTITY:** You are The CARER which means that you like to show your love and compassion to others through your relationships a well as in your work.

**MY PURPOSE:** You are The CARER and are very good in understanding people, especially those who need help such as patients, clients, family and colleagues. By speaking with your love and feelings, you can touch people's hearts in ways that many others cannot. You also express yourself through artistic and beautiful ways that are unique to the Carer.

# The Giver

**MY TALENT:** As the GIVER, you easily sense other people's needs, especially those who need help. You are generous with your time and money, often putting your own needs aside. You are a positive, energetic person who will do anything for your family and friends and those you care for. Loving and helping people at home, work, school, charities, etc is your calling and it makes you feel appreciated.

**MY ATTRACTION:** People are attracted to you when you show your loving KINDNESS to them by helping them. You relate easily with others though your warmth and friendliness. Ephesians 4:22 could your motto: "Be kind and loving to each other. Forgive each other the same as God forgave you through Christ." Because you don't know if you could be talking to someone , who's trying their best not to fall apart.

**MY IDENTITY:** Your identity is the GIVER. meaning that you find your identity in helping people and bring hope to others for the future, by supporting people and building their confidence.

**MY PURPOSE:** While you are not an out-there person, you have a gift for getting beside people and helping to support them. You have a gift for building relationships with people by showing your empathy, love, and encouragement. Your purpose and appreciation is your kindness.

I am a loyal and faithful person who likes belonging to a close group of friends and colleagues. I take longer to make decisions, so I don't make mistakes. I am good at doing tasks properly.

☐ I like to know the rules
☐ I see what can go wrong
☐ I like being in a team
☐ I like to get all the details
☐ I am reliable & trustworthy
☐ I follow instructions
☐ I like predictability

*If you have more ticks above, tick the box below.*

☐ I am
a **Planner**

*Turn to page 73*

I am more academic and enjoy studying and learning new knowledge. I collect information and facts so that I can analyse them and find new solutions to problems.

☐ I'm analytical
☐ I collect information
☐ I'm observational
☐ I want to understand
☐ Builds & tests theories
☐ Presents explanations
☐ Connects facts

*If you have more ticks above, tick the box below.*

☐ I am
a **Researcher**

*Turn to page 74*

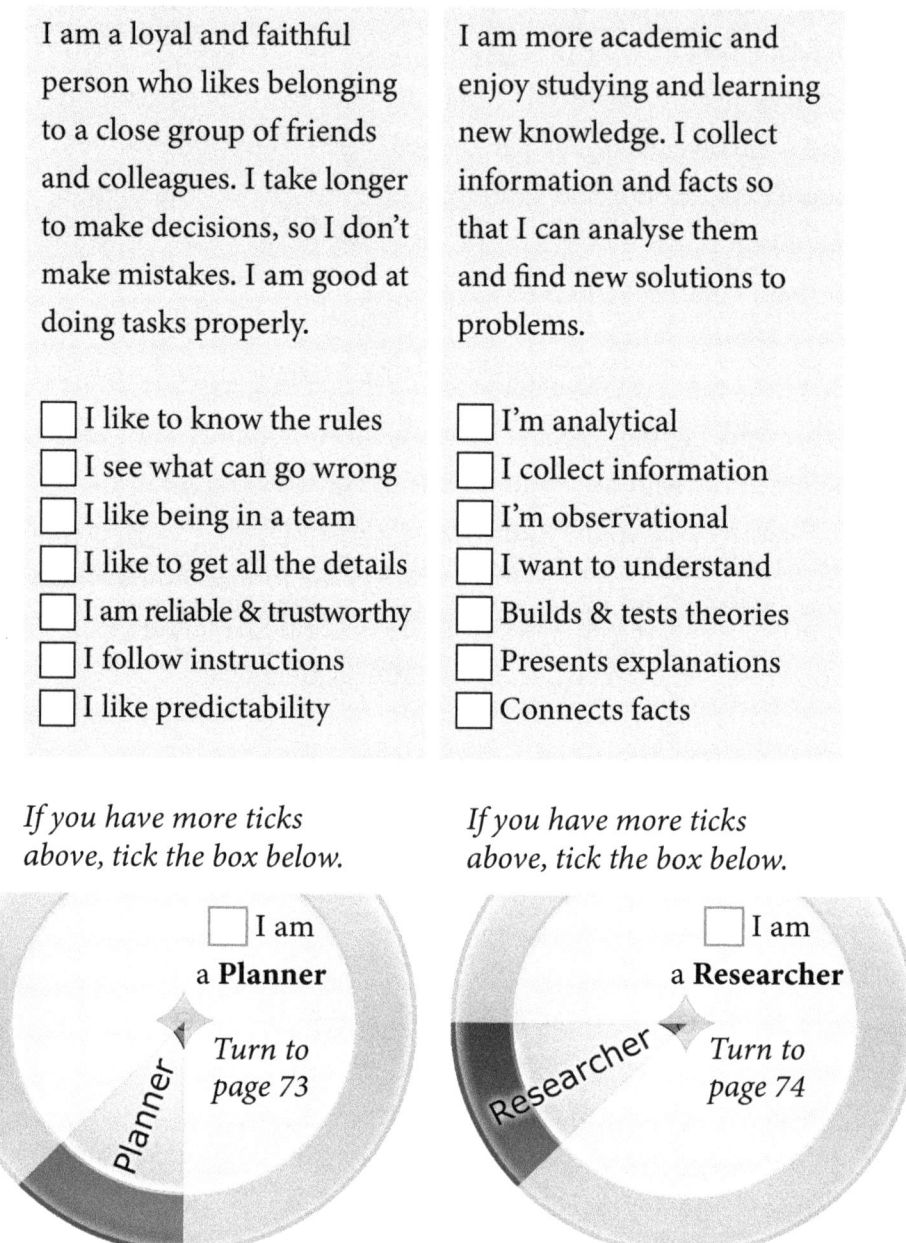

# The Planner

**MY TALENT:** You are a practical person who has or is able to acquire a skill and mastery at tasks, big or small. You are more concerned with doing something practical than with theories and ideas. You may take longer to make decisions because you like to get all the details first, so that you don't make mistakes. This is why you are skilled at tasks that have to be done properly and accurately. You function well when you know what you have to do or have proper guidelines and instructions. You will work hard to do the job well and to finish the jobs you are given.

**MY ATTRACTION:** Your attraction is that you relate with people as a loyal and faithful person who likes belonging to a close group of friends and colleagues. You like to serve and support your family and close friends. You are trustworthy, responsible and reliable.

**MY IDENTITY:** You are a Practical person who can put things into practice to accomplish your tasks.

**MY PURPOSE:** You have a natural functional ability to do a task well by following your training and the instructions. Your natural practical skills allows you to operate as a task person to fulfill your purpose.

# The Researcher

**MY TALENT:** You are an intellectual person who enjoys studying, researching and learning new knowledge. Being a critical thinker, you can think both inside and outside the box. This enables you to analyse data to research and discover new methods and strategies. You like to observe, question and analyse problems, to build frameworks to explain theories, and develop systems and models to demonstrate what is happening in particular situations.

**MY ATTRACTION:** You may have a gentle nature in your relating with people as you like to be calm and in control of your emotions. People are attracted to your knowledge and appreciate your wisdom.

**MY IDENTITY:** You are The Intellectual who is a specialist in the knowledge of a subject or subjects. As a thinker you like to study, examine and research subjects in detail, develop strategies and make recommendations by breaking information into smaller parts to come up with an explanation.

**MY PURPOSE:** As a knowledge person you feel your purpose is to know and understand as much as possible within the boundaries of your specialisation. Your relaxation and relationships could also be similar in that you and others may find an outlet for a hobby that becomes a passionate project An example might be an extensive miniature railway network, or a regular card game in your neighbourhood.

I like managing people and projects. I like maintaining correct standards to get the best out of people. I use both logic and facts to get the job done on budget and on time.

- [ ] I am reliable & punctual
- [ ] I am self–disciplined
- [ ] I am logical & realistic
- [ ] I like to be organized
- [ ] Problem solving
- [ ] Integrity is important
- [ ] I see things as right/wrong

*If you have more ticks above, tick the box below.*

I like to be in control to get the best results. I don't avoid conflict or confrontation and have a strong sense of justice and fair play. I am not slow to make the decisions to get things done.

- [ ] I like new challenges
- [ ] I make the decisions
- [ ] I embrace change
- [ ] I don't avoid conflict
- [ ] I am a confident leader
- [ ] I respect those who stand up
- [ ] I like to be in charge

*If you have more ticks above, tick the box below.*

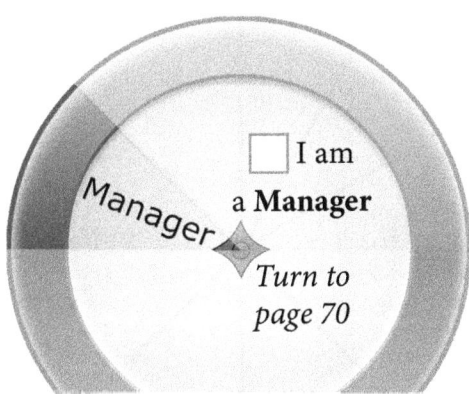

Manager

- [ ] I am a **Manager**

*Turn to page 70*

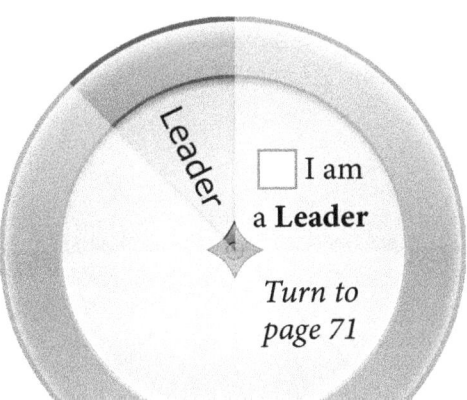

Leader

- [ ] I am a **Leader**

*Turn to page 71*

# The Manager

**MY TALENT:** You are a logical person and good at managing and administering both people and projects. You are concerned about maintaining correct standards and you like to get the best out of people and projects. You are responsible and self-disciplined to get the job done on budget and on time, while taking into account the concerns of people that you manage.

**MY ATTRACTION:** You like to relate with others in the correct ways, to do what is right at the right time in the right way. People respect and trust you and you make them feel comfortable and secure. You respect others and do the right thing—the little things that really matter, like being on time, being honest, being reliable, etc, You use logic to manage projects and to make the big decisions.

**MY IDENTITY:** The Manager– you make a good manager of both people and projects with your ability to build up and train people in the right way to go.

**MY PURPOSE:** Is to manage by good communication with all people including family, friends, colleagues, clients and partners, by strong leadership, while showing empathy and accountability.

# The Leader

**MY TALENT:** You are a confident and assertive leader who likes being in control and to take direct action. You don't avoid facing conflict and confrontation. You have a strong sense of justice and fair play. You focus mainly on projects and expect people to follow your directions. You like to get the facts, choose the best course of action and get the best results.

**MY ATTRACTION:** You are naturally a charismatic person as you are born with such strong gifts and talents. People are attracted to your strong and confident character and your ability to talk well as you are naturally smart in having verbal, linguistic intelligence. This means that you can hold your own in most conversations. However, you have to use self control as your strengths are strong and you will need self-control so as not to dominate, and cause hurt.

**MY IDENTITY:** You are the Leader. You are the person who naturally takes charge and commands a country, organisation, team or any group of people or projects. Leaders often prefer leading projects to leading people, but most often it is both.

**MY PURPOSE:** Is to know that you are born to lead and you are not afraid to step up when needed. Most people prefer to follow as making decisions is harder for them. However, you have the natural ability to want to make decisions and to put it into action.

Now that we have discovered your main talent, it's now time to think about what is your second talent, just as we did for your personality.

Your second talent is very important as it shapes and directs how you will use your first talent.

Go back over the previous pages and make a note of the talent that is also like you.

You can make a note here of your talents:

My main talent is _____

My secondary talent is _____

# PART 4

# Real Life Stories About Gifted and Talented People

## Real Life Stories from each Personality

This part of the book is really interesting as we begin with the story of a real person who has that particular Personality Type. My hunch is that as you read their stories, each Personality will come to life. Some will resonate deeply with you – they'll be like a mirror to you, reflecting who you are. Others won't, but you'll probably recognise someone you know in each story. So each of the nine personalities takes a similar form that looks something like this:

- A real life story from a person from each personality type
- A section called "Who or what is this Personality"
- A short section explaining how and why this Personality Type is motivated first and foremost through the soul, the heart, the mind or the will
- An explanation of why the rest of us need this Personality Type – this is their value proposition to the rest of us, to help us appreciate who they are and what they have to offer.

So there's a lot there in each of the next nine chapters. May the Lord use it to help you understand yourself, to help you understand the people around you and to lift you up to be all that He planned for you to be. Does this sound vaguely familiar? Even though we know we are all different, most people really acts as though "normal" equals "being like me".

Through their life stories, each of these Personalities come to life. Their stories were just remarkable – and what is really amazing is how incredibly different they were. At the book launch we asked each of them basically the same questions, and yet the answers were so radically different. And yet we tend to superimpose our own outlook on life, onto them. That's our default position. We imagine that our family, friends, etc see the world the way we do – and let me tell you, they just don't. Now we kind of know that, but we behave as though they're just like us and then when they're not we wonder why?

## Len's Story - The Achiever

For over thirty-seven years I've had various roles, primarily with a sales orientation: anything from running major accounts, working for big organisations like IBM, handling major projects. One of the largest projects I was involved with was a defence department re-equipment of their whole logistics area which is everything from tanks to toilet paper. It was the largest systems project that IBM had ever undertaken in this country. Those kind of projects, are in capital equipment sales, but always in that world of solution selling.

That's given me opportunities to move rapidly through organisations where I've ended up running sales operations at state and country level in various companies I guess that the whole achievement, recognition, rewards thing has always been something that's motivated me; to have the opportunity to stand out from the crowd. Mostly, it's just competing against myself. Just to be there up front, having won the recognitions along the way, various wonderful trips. Although just recently I've come back from a wonderful trip with my wife to Mexico, which I received because I was the top achiever for the Asia Pacific Region for the company that I was working with.

And it's not just in my work life – I have this energy. Time off is something I don't really do. The trouble is I often feel guilty when I'm not doing something If a day goes by and I haven't been able to tick something off to say I've done something, I feel like the day is wasted. One of the things I don't like doing; that I'm not good at, is being micro managed. And when somebody says "You've got to fit into this mould and make it work this way", it's really quite frustrating. So I don't like that. But strangely enough, while I love my independence, I do like working with teams. I love working with a team, provided they don't want to own me 24/7. If I can "put into them" – invest in them, motivate them and give them something that helps them do what they do, that's what I love. But then, leave me alone, I want to do what I want to do. Let me go and achieve what I want to achieve now! Does that make sense?

So – heavy accountability, administrative bureaucracy – those things absolutely drive me nuts. They stifle me. They stop me from achieving results. I tend to have a detailed orientation because I make meaning out of putting the pieces together.

**What does it mean when one person encourages another?**

Enter the Achieving Encourager, or "The Achiever" as we've called them. When you look at it that way, you can see how Len is a classic Achiever. Not only does he achieve in his own life, but he also has a real heart for helping other people to achieve as well – that's the Encouraging side of the Achiever. That's why he's managed sales teams. That's why he's been successful in selling and managing everything from information technology solutions, large and small, through to earthmoving equipment. He achieves in his own life, but he also encourages other people to achieve. He's a go-get-it, can-do person who by his very nature inspires confidence in others. He can't help himself. People get around him, and they're just lifted up to achieve. They start to feel good about themselves and that inspires them to succeed. Len's both positive and people-oriented. He loves to win and help other people to win. That's why he's inspirational. He can keep going when other people have long given up – because he wants to win; he wants to achieve. That's why people think of Len as a workaholic. Here is your classic Achiever.

**Who or What Is the "Achiever"?**

I always like to bring these Personality Types back to what God's Word says – so let's have another look: We have gifts that differ according to the grace given to us: prophecy, in proportion to faith; ministry, in ministering; the teacher, in teaching; the exhorter, in exhortation; the giver, in generosity; the leader, in diligence; the compassionate, in cheerfulness. (Romans 12:6-8) I mentioned earlier, that whilst Romans Chapter 12 talks about seven Personalities, we'd expanded that into nine, meaning we'd taken two of the seven and split each of those two in two (if that makes sense) giving us a total of nine.

The first one with which we've split is the Encourager. And that's because there are two distinctly different types of Encouragers. The first is like Len – the "Achieving Encourager" and the second is like Tom – the "Social Encourager". We'll meet Tom next and one of the things we'll discover about him is that even though on the one hand he is an Encourager like Len, on the other, achieving is not necessarily the first priority for him. So whilst these two are both truly Encouragers, just one of them is focused on achievement (can't miss that, having met Len now, can we?) – and to keep it simple, we've called this Personality Type "The Achiever".

The other Personality Type is "The Encourager". Make sense? Now this may seem a little odd, but I want to unpack the meaning of the word "encouragement" as some translations render it, here in Romans 12:8, because whenever we dig deep into God's Word, a light shines out to illuminate our subject matter. That's always the way with God's Word. And the original Greek word that Paul uses here for "Encourager" is the same word, the very same word that Jesus uses to describe the Holy Spirit to His Disciples (John 14:16), although Paul uses it as a verb and Jesus as a noun.

Nevertheless, it's the same word, that word is parable (that's the verb, parakletos being the noun) which means to beseech, to exhort, to encourage, to strengthen and to comfort. So here we have this sense of a couple of Personality Types who are prone to draw alongside us, just like God Himself through the Holy Spirit, in order to beseech, to exhort, to encourage, to strengthen and to comfort us. Isn't that powerful? What a wonderful picture of encouragement! So have you ever asked yourself – exactly what is encouragement?

## Why Is the Achiever Motivated Through the Soul?

Do you notice how Len achieves by exercising his will, his drive, his determination. Do you see how he likes order – he succeeds by using his mind to put the pieces together and make sense out of them. And do you see how he has a heart to lift other people up, to inspire and empower teams of people to achieve? These people use their will, their mind and their heart to be who God made them to be. That's why the Achiever is here in the "soul" quadrant. They approach life holistically – with their whole soul – rather than predominantly through their heart or their mind or their will.

## Why Do the Rest of Us Need the Achiever?

Firstly, they drive themselves hard and achieve things. Doesn't matter what team we're on, we need Achievers to make things happen. We can rely on them to set goals, and tick each one off – they get things done. Secondly, they motivate the rest of us to get things done. There are some Personality Types (we'll meet them a little later) for whom, to put it mildly, getting things done is not their first love nor is it their particular forté in life. Sure, they have other strengths, but we all need to get things done.

## Tom's Story - The Encourager

Tom is an Encourager. You can sense that about him after just a few minutes. He makes you feel at ease; he makes you feel good about yourself. He's the sort of person we'd all enjoy having coffee with. Here's Tom's story, as told by him. So, what does Tom do?

"Well, I actually fell into photography. I found that this is something I love doing. I thought to myself 'I'll do photography for a little while and then I'll move on and try other things.' But that wasn't to be. I like expressing myself visually and I find that God expresses Himself through what I do. And I think that really encourages people to look at something a little bit differently. This is not just a normal photograph. They're seeing something which is unique and unusual and I think that's the gift that I've been given – a gift that allows people visually to see God.

You asked me what I'd love to do if I had an hour or so to myself – aside from the fact that I have two young kids and that is never going to happen – but if I had a couple of hours to myself what would I do? I really couldn't decide. Truly. I could probably think of twenty different things and I'd want to do them all in that couple of hours. But then I'd probably end up going, 'No, I'm going to get some sleep.'
If you asked me 'What drives me nuts about people?' I would say that there's not many things that would annoy me. I love

people, I'm not the sort of person who would judge someone instantly. I trust everybody. I'm always open to love everybody rather than seeing the bad in people. As soon as I meet someone, I instantly want to be their friend, if that makes sense. I always feel like I want to know people, like I've known them for a long time rather than having just met them."

"I had been a photographer for 4 years and could just see my life and career were headed nowhere and what he needed to do was focus. I was just about to spend a lot of money on a business mentor because I thought that my business had to go the next step but I didn't know how. I said to Keith, 'I'm looking at hiring a business mentor" and he said 'Why don't we catch up and maybe I can help you out.' So I thought, 'What a blessing. Fantastic!'

When we began catching up I said 'Okay, this photography thing is what I want to do for the next five years. And then I'm going to do this, and then this, and then this.' I'd had this plan in my mind for so long that this is exactly what I was going to do. But when Keith came out and said, 'Actually, no! You're not going to do that,' it threw me like you wouldn't believe. It was a real turning point in my life. 'No, photography is your gift. It's your ministry, it's what God gave you to do.' ...
That was a complete turning point in my life. And as soon as I focused, everything just fell into place, I actually bought a new car and then I actually decided to go buy a house and my business just roared along and now I have four part-time staff that work from the studio.

If you'd told me three years ago that this was going to happen, I would have gone 'No, that's not going to happen. I'm going to do this, this and this.'"

## Who or What Is the "Encourager"?

While Romans Chapter 12 talks about a single gift of encouragement (or exhortation) – in the "GPS" tool we've broken that gift into two separate Personality Types: the Achieving Encourager (the "Achiever") and the Social Encourager (the "Encourager"). When we met Len, the Achiever and Tom the Encourager, we can see how in one sense they're very much alike, but in another sense, they're entirely different. They're both Encouragers – but in quite different ways. Len encourages people to achieve things as a big picture Soul/Will person– he gets them on their bike and heading down the road and he helps them stay on the track. But did you notice as Tom told his story, how different he is? Achieving anything was creativity. He is a Soul/Mind person with visual intelligence. Tom wanted to experience all the different options. He wanted to have fun. He's the guy on a long journey who wants to stop for a swim and an ice cream. Who cares when we get there, let's enjoy the journey. I'll do this for a few years, and then I'll do that for a few years. Seems that the Encourager is never short of options. And there's a reason for that. Everybody likes having them around – that's why. They always have friends, they always have an invitation to go out on Friday night, or to have coffee during the week.

And with all those connections and relationships, naturally, come lots of options. Tom's world generally doesn't have too much difficulty finding a job – because employers meets them, likes them and hires them. The problem they have to sticking with a job and seeing things through. But in the meantime ... in the meantime they're having fun. They feel good about themselves and they make the rest of us feel good about ourselves too.

## Why Is the Encourager Motivated Through the Soul?

Now first up when you listen to Tom tell his story, you get the impression that he leads with his heart. He follows his emotions and his desires. After all, it's about having fun. This feels good, let's do this. Oh – look at that over there. That looks good. Let's give that a go. It's about what feels good. But notice what happens when Keith whacks Tom over the head with a lump of four-by-two. When someone finally points out to him that he lacks focus and that he'll succeed if he gets focused on one thing – what happens? Effortlessly it seems, the Encourager gets focused. Starting a small business and getting it to succeed requires drive, energy, will power. It requires a lot of detail to be dealt with and managed. Tom's photography business required all three – the heart, the mind and the will. And without too much trouble, Tom was able to bring all three to the table. That's why Encouragers are invariably pretty good at whatever they turn their hands to. Because they can use their heart, their mind and their will. And once they focus, they're good at whatever it is that they're doing. Now a wedding photography business seems an odd business for an Encourager to go into. But think about it. Tom has a special gift for taking photos that captivate us. Wedding days are pretty full-on and stressful for the bride and groom. What better person to have taking their photos than an Encourager – someone who makes them feel good? It's just like an Encourager to land on his feet like that.

## Why Do the Rest of Us Need the Encourager?

Do you remember back when we were looking at Len the Achiever, we talked about the fact that encouragement is about filling another person with confidence? And where the Achiever fills us with confidence about what we can do – so that we too can achieve things, the Encourager fills us with confidence about who we are. They bring optimism to our lives. They take us out of our own inner world where we can be thinking negative thoughts, where we feel sometimes that we have little or no worth, where we imagine that there is no future for us – and they light up our inner world and reflect a sense of value and worth into our lives. That's why we just like being around them. And that's why the rest of us need them around.

## Malcom's Story - The Mentor

I do a few things with my life. I do this recording for a radio program. That's the solitary part of what I do. Most of the time, I'm watching you through the glass panel in the studio and then it's hours on my own, editing and producing the programs. I'm also involved in the music and worship team at our church, and I'm the Mentor involved in ministry outside of church. I'm part of the music and worship team there as well. So, it's a whole range of things. I really love to pull alongside people and spend time with them. It's kind of the life-coach model. It's the joy of guiding people threw their problems and seeing God setting them free.

I've been trained as a counsellor and I love doing that. When it comes to spending time just for me, my favourite thing is getting into my sea kayak and go paddling out in the ocean. And then I have my bees to look after – they make great honey – in fact selling the honey is what gave me the money to buy the sea kayak. But really, I enjoy people. I think I've always enjoyed people. Maybe that's not true. I know I hated crowds when I was a kid. To go to a thing like the Royal Easter Show or something in Sydney, that was the last place on Earth that I would want to be as a kid. I'm okay with it now, but one to one, small groups – I enjoy that. Even to have a crowd of six or ten or forty people over for a party is really hard work for me. But two or three, I love it. I can pull alongside and connect with them. I want to help them to see God more clearly. They have the ability within them to connect with God or to receive the connection that God's already giving them. And to work their way through the issues that they're dealing with. I love doing it. I don't feel particularly unique or special. I know there are some areas that I cope with better than others. For instance, many of the people I know don't cope as well with others doing or saying things around them that they disagree with. I do, it doesn't bother me and I don't understand why others aren't like that. In that sense, when I look at other people, yes, they have issues with something that was said, and I think "What's the problem?" I guess you could say I was easy-going. Things just don't seem to upset me.

## Who or What Is the "Mentor"?

In Romans 12 they are called The Teacher, however when we run a workshop hardly anyone recognises themselves as the Teacher, mainly because they don't teach at a school. So we changed their name to the Mentor, because that is what a teacher does, they support and Mentor the students in their learning. Jesus was as much a "mentor" and "life coach" to the disciples as He was preacher. In so-called primitive societies, the most important function of the older men, was to teach the boys how to become men. Why? Because the tribe's future depends on it – on this male mentorship and on teaching about life. There is a wonderful quote from a woman who'd moved from Poland to America after World War II – and she said: "Back in Poland we didn't have therapists. We had friends." That's what Mentors do, they have a heart to pull alongside others in and to make a difference by being there to speak wisdom and truth into others' lives.

## Why Is the Mentor Motivated through the Soul?

Let's go back to Malcolm's story for a moment. I imagine that the people he counsels, many of whom are damaged or hurting – are all different. Some of them will be emotional – seeing and experiencing the world through their hearts, above everything else. Others will be Mind people. And others again, will be people who operate from the strength of their Will. If the Mentor is going to connect with each of those, they need to adjust to be able to connect with people, whether they operate from their Heart, their Mind or their Will. in bringing transformation.

## Why do the rest of us Need the Mentor?

It's amazing how clearly we are able to see and judge other people's faults, but we cut ourselves a whole bunch more slack, when it comes to our own. And those faults are like chains that bind us and enslave us. They can rob us of the fullness of life, the joy and the peace that God has planned for us. That's why He calls them sin. And that's why He sent His Son to set us free. But you and I – we're prone to holding onto that sin for grim death (pun intended). It takes a special person to pull alongside and "stab us in the front" in a way that we can accept; in a way that brings transformation. Enter ... the Mentor.

## Anne's Story - The Carer

What I've found for most of my life, is that people tend to come to me when they have problems. Basically I'm the one that they come to because they know that I will always listen and I care about them if they're hurting. And I hurt for them as well because I feel it with them; I have empathy for people. I'm very much a friend-orientated kind of person. Relationships and friendships really, really matter to me. I live out my faith I think, by being available to people – to talk with them and journey with them through their lives – all the ups and downs. And I also love doing things for people as well, whether it's calling them up and seeing if they are okay or baking someone a cake or just making them feel better – that's my aim. I love it.

I guess I feel different to other people. I do, because I see that they don't care as much about relationships as I do. I find it very easy to get offended by the way people act around me if I perceive them as not caring enough about me or doing things that may offend me – even if to them they're just a different personality so they think a different way. So it doesn't mean the same thing to them. But to me I have to be really careful of not interpreting things as someone specifically doing something to hurt me. Things that I'm not so good at? Hmm. I'm not so good at thinking in the big picture, long term. I tend to get overwhelmed very easily. So I'm a lot better at living day-to-day than trying to look too far ahead into the future. I love doing stuff for people, making them feel happy and helping them sort through their problems. But I also find it really hard if they don't appreciate what I do. Most of all I need to be acknowledged and appreciated. Which is a weakness, something I have to be careful of but it's part of who I am. Allowing my feelings to be hurt by other people is something I have to be very careful of. Even though it's a good thing because you have empathy for other people, it can be a very bad thing too because you can get hurt and depressed very easily. Basically that happens because a situation can happen and a day goes by, a week goes by and I'm still thinking about it in my head. And I can very easily make it into something that it wasn't. So a lot of the time I go very inwards; into my emotions, and into my thoughts and if I'm not careful, it very quickly spirals into depression.

**Who or What Is the "Carer"?**

The Carer comes from the heart, emotions – and that's something we've seen either in ourselves or in other people, so it's something we can readily understand – whether we're a heart person or not. Now this particular Personality Type is referred to here as the compassionate one. It means literally to have mercy, to help someone who is afflicted or seeking aid, to help someone who is in desperate need. We saw that in Anne's story too, didn't we? What I've found for most of my life, is that people tend to come to me when they have problems. Basically I'm the one that they come to because they know that I will always listen and I care about them if they're hurting ... And what a wonderful way for God to make someone! What a wonderful purpose for God to give someone in their lives!

## Why Is the Carer Motivated Through the Heart?

It may be that you or I are motivated primarily by a part of us other than our hearts. But when we are broken hearted – we need someone who can reach our heart, don't we? We need someone who can feel with us, hurt with us, cry with us and touch our emotions and touch our heart in a healing way. And it doesn't have to be some devastating, cataclysmic situation which tears our hearts apart either. Just in the rough and tumble of the day, our hearts can be bruised – our emotions hurt. Whatever it is, however, big or small, when our heart aches, right at that moment, we need someone who knows how to speak our heart-language, because that's the part of us that needs speaking to. And so it's pretty much self-evident why Carers are motivated first and foremost through their emotions.

## Why do the rest of us need the Carer?

Can you imagine a professional football team without a team doctor? Can you imagine a world devoid of Carers? It would be a pretty cold and bleak place, wouldn't it? When our heart aches, we don't need an Achiever to inspire us on to greater achievements. We don't so much need an Encourager to make us feel good either. Nor do we need a Mentor right at that point of our injury – what we need right at that moment is the Carer – someone who can bind up the broken hearted. That's why people naturally go to Anne when they're hurting. Her personality hangs out an "Aid Station" sign that people can't miss.

## Ava's Story - The Giver

I've always been involved in administration work for the last 25 years or so. My husband and I have been in business together. He's the one that's out there with all the ideas and doing things and I'm the one who puts it together. I come along behind him – while he's out there having new ideas and creating new opportunities, I make it happen at the back end. Does that make sense? We're different but it works well together. And in the past, I've done a lot of school administration work and church administration work. the Giver. I like to get beside somebody, working on a project with them, working on a task. Watching things like that get done, in a family area, at work, whatever. Doing things with people and for people. Just getting beside them and helping them and making sure they're okay.

I heard you ask the other people in the studio before me about the things they don't like doing. And I've been thinking about that. The thing I don't like doing is getting up in front of a group of people and speaking. It's just – well, it's just not me. It's not what I do. I've always found that being up front and speaking is very hard for me, which has been a challenge, but I actually have been able to overcome it little by little, I think with the Lord's help. What really annoys me about other people? That's easy. When they don't pitch in and help. When they just stand there and watch other people working. So it really frustrates me when people wait for others to do things. I just don't understand how you can do that. I'm starting to learn that other people think differently. And I also understand my own limitations. I'm not out there into the big picture like my husband is. I'd rather just be working and making things happen. You know, getting down and helping. Behind the scenes – getting beside people but more on a one-to-one basis, not in a big group. Basically, I like to look after people. When you see somebody who needs a little bit of help, someone who's struggling. At the moment we have young grand children and our kids really need a hand. I love doing that and I love to just sit and chat with them and make sure everything's going okay.

## Who or What Is the "Giver"?

In an increasingly materialistic society, where the desire for wealth and consumerism are that most people associate the notion of giving purely with money. The Greek word for the Giver means very simply to give or to impart. Giving in a community where people rely on one another, means to help each other, to meet one another's physical needs. To look after someone's children while the parents are working. To cook a meal for someone when they are ill. To help an elderly neighbour, Whilst the Carer meets someone's emotional needs, the Giver is motivated to meet their physical needs. You can see the stark contrast between the Carer and the Giver in the story of Mary and Martha, in the New Testament: Now as they went on their way, he [Jesus] entered a certain village, where a woman named Martha welcomed him into her home. She had a sister named Mary, who sat at the Lord's feet and listened to what he was saying. But Martha was distracted by her many tasks; so she came to him and asked, "Lord, do you not care that my sister has left me to do all the work by myself? Tell her then to help me." (Luke 10:38-40) Martha is the classic

Giver. She expresses her love and her faith through practical acts of service and assistance. Mary on the other hand is more captivated by the relationship with Jesus. She sits at His feet. Whilst Martha is the Giver, Mary is more likely the Carer.

**Why Is the Giver Motivated Through the Heart?**

They see other people's needs, and they're moved in their heart. They simply cannot see a need go unmet. The needs that they feel in their heart, they want to meet with their hands. If others had to exercise their will every time there was a need to be met, it would be exhausting for them or a challenge for them. But because they feel it in their hearts, it's the most natural thing in the world for them. And they simply can't understand what's wrong with the rest of us.

Why Do the Rest of Us Need the Giver?

The easiest thing in the world, is to sit back and let the Giver do all the work. We can just leave all the doing up to them. But we do need the Givers around because they do something that the rest of us aren't wired to do. Since for them this is a heart thing, they instantly make a connection between a heart-felt physical need, and the action that's required to meet that need.

## Lewis's Story - The Planner

I do a whole range of things, I suppose, in my life. I work
a lot in detailed design and do a lot of creative things but
there is also the practical side. I work with a small company,
and I'm pretty much the product manager. So, I oversee the
development of the products and the packaging and design.
It's really thinking through how things are going to work over
a long period of time and what the outcome's going to be
and how it's all going to tie in together. So, in a nutshell, I'm
the one who designs the products that we're going to take to
market.

At work, people really come to me to help them nut things out
– figure the Planner. To work through the issues that'll make
things work ... whether it's over the website, or products. It's
always the finer details of accounting or anything else we're
trying to work out. They can't always get their head around it,
but it's really easy for me to do.

So, I guess I'm the detail "go-to" guy. And in my spare time,
I like to go for a surf. Having a bit of time out is always good
because I'm a thinker. It's good to get away from that and have
some time out to myself. Things tick over in my head and I get
through things when I'm on my own. So, any quiet time where
I can be alone and I can think and not be overwhelmed by
everything else.

What drives me nuts about other people? Well, a big realisation for me, I've always found it hard with people that are not doing the things that I can see that need to be done. I'm always thinking and seeing how I can help out and what I can do, but other people, they're either in a group chatting or they're doing different things but they're not taking care of those things that I can see. They can't see the detail and so I have to run around and do everything, so I wonder – why isn't everyone else helping out? Why don't they get it?

But at the same time, the thing I really struggle with is that I get overwhelmed when too much is happening at once. I need to do one thing at a time. So, I've got to be focusing on one thing, I can't be spreading myself out trying to do lots of different things. So that's always hard for me. I just concentrate on one thing. At our church I'm the head of the video ministry so I'm always behind the scenes doing different bits and pieces, setting up cameras and editing and doing the odds and ends. I'm the person behind the scenes. Sometimes it's not recognised, sometimes it is. For me I usually prefer not to be recognised.

It's nice to be behind the scenes, to be humble and not to be out the front. So that's the sort of place I fit in and makes me feel at home. It's using what my gifts are, it's also having to think ahead and get things planned and get it all together. It's good to be a part of the team. That's when you find real fulfilment, when you know exactly who you are and you're putting that into practice. Skilled Servers think through the detail and get on and do things by solving practical problems in a way that the rest of us just can't.

**Who or What Is the Planner**

Now the easiest thing in the world for me to do is to get the Planner mixed up with the Giver. When you understand the Giver, you see that they like doing things for people. Turns out, that the Planner is quite a "doer" too – But they're also quite different actually – because the Giver comes from the Heart and the Skilled Server comes from the Mind. That's why in the "God's Personality System" tool, we've broken that one type of Encourager into two Personality Types. Well in the same way we've taken this gift of "serving" which is more literally what the original Greek word means – and broken it into two Personality Types. But in essence, both come from the same place – the desire and motivation and ability to use their mind to think through the detail. The only thing that's different really, is the outcome. And with the Planner, the outcome of thinking through all that detail, is a practical solution. A product. A website. A building. A video. You can see that in Lewis's story.

## Why Is the Planner Motivated Through the Mind?

Did you notice how Lewis explained things? He thinks through things. He sees the detail when others don't and then he thinks things through and makes them happen. He naturally sees the detail and has the ability to use his mind to work his way through it and come up with a practical solution. There was a young man by the name of Adam who was the onsite foreman and lead carpenter on our build. And you could see why he had that job. I remember one particularly complex part of the roof where all these different angles and parts had to come together. No one could visualise it. Not Adam, certainly not me and even the master builder couldn't visualise how it was going to work. But Adam had a quiet confidence and said to the rest of us, "Just give it a couple of days and I'll figure it out." And he did. And it ended up looking sensational. These people – these Skillful people – think through problems to create solutions that the rest of us can't readily see.

Why do the rest of us need a Practical person?

Without Lewis, the company he works for simply wouldn't function as well, because much of the detail would be lost and in the complexity of all that they do, things simply wouldn't come together in a way that works. And without Lewis, neither would the video ministry in his church quietly come together the way it does today. And without Adam, my house renovation would never have been completed. I could never have done what he did.

## James Story - The Researcher

I've been a Christian minister and been involved in universities too, and I find that I tend to react against being too involved in an institution. I like to observe, I find that I can very easily just stand on my own and look at things and be pleasant and my instinct, my natural personality would be to just be on my own. I'm a loner – I'm just happy to be that way. But as part of my Christian life and my Christian commitment I realised that the body life of the church means that I had to learn how to relate and to be nice to people. But honestly, reading books and being on my own is what I really like.

So, this knowledge thing can become a trap because you can be so interested. I could walk into a bookshop and I would systematically work my way around the shop and pick up anything that I thought was interesting. After a while I realised I was just going in ten different directions at the same time. I don't want to do that. I want to be able to focus and get my life going in a direction that I think is a Christian responsibility; to come against this attraction to knowledge and going off in all directions. So, I've got my own library; I focus on the interests that I have. I've been a Bible teacher too and one of the things that I do is focus on Scripture and I want to tease it out, I mean to the Greek and the Hebrew and I have opportunities within the church to be able to teach that. It's important to me to serve and to interact where I live out my faith.

I preach and I've got that kind of profile within the church which is a kind of leadership. Not a management type but observation type leadership where things are happening and I can come in and say, "Well, is this the right thing that we should be doing?"The one thing I don't like to do? I don't like just plain entertainment or plain fun. People just like the fun. At home I can use the word 'fun' in a negative way, where they're using it in a positive way. You're just having 'fun'. What are you doing? What is the point of what you're doing? So, one of the things I don't like doing is to live an unreflective life. Researchers live for the sake of thinking and researching, more than they do for the purpose of creating a practical outcome.

## Who or What Is the Researcher?

The reason that we have separated the Mind personality into two parts, is because there are two very distinctly different thinkers. While they are both mind personalities the Planner is a doing, hands-on, task person as the Intellectual researches to be able to understand and to be knowledgeable in their specialist field and like to have time being alone to study, research and analyse problems and develop new solutions.

## Why Do the Rest of Us Need the Researcher?

The reason we need the Intellectuals is for their deep knowledge and understanding of complex problems through their time-consuming research. They make good researchers as you don't easily get distracted, are not emotionally persuaded and can stay with a problem for a very long time till they find the solution. They are like a forensic lawyer who searches deeply to gather all the facts using scientific methods and techniques to investigate. A lot of Intelletuals would have been involved in developing the vaccines and medicines to fight the Covid 19 epidemic and other medical needs.

**Why Is the Researcher person motivated through the Mind?**

Well, that is just so blindingly obvious! It's all about the mind for the Thinker. Could you imagine any other Personality Type that we've investigated so far, doing what these scientists have done – armies of them have given us the technology that we take for granted today? The mind is indeed a powerful thing. Their thinking style is analytical, meaning that these people are smart at researching and analysing problems at a much deeper level than the other personalities. They are focused about finding the meaning of complex problems and coming up with a solution. They make good researchers and inventors as they not only use existing knowledge but also take in information from their environment, other research, including new ideas, new evidence, etc. Yet they can change their mind if new evidence becomes available.

## Gary's Story – The Manager

What do I do, well as a husband and a father of 4 school aged children, I don't have a lot of spare time. A lot of weekends is taken up with sport, church and our family. At work I am also a partner in a busy accountancy practice in Sydney, working mainly with businesses advising them on tax, regulations, structures, etc that may affect them. You could say that I lead a full and satisfying life.

What do I like doing? I really enjoy working with people and I get a lot of satisfaction out of advising and helping solve their accounting and financial challenges, working on projects and just helping people. For instance, when I was going to university and through my early working life, I also ran a youth group for teenagers. I really enjoyed this, working with teenagers and helping the youth grow up into strong Christians and future leaders.

How is my personality different from others? I am from the Will which means I like to manage and drive projects and to see the results. I spend most of my work time solving problems and giving advice. Which also applies in my family life and the many decisions we all make as a family. I naturally see things in more logical ways and can sense what is the right way or the wrong. I believe we should all try and to do the right thing by each other. I have a strong sense of integrity and try to uphold my values in everything that I do. One thing about being a Manager is that I was born with good self- discipline which helps me to focus on what I am doing and to get it done. This is valuable for my work and family and in relationships with others. I also enjoy sports and used to play tennis but these days I mainly enjoy taking our children to their sports and watching them play.

What drives me nuts about people? Not really a lot, but possibly people who promise they will do something and then let you down by not doing it.

**Who or What Is the "Manager"?**

What we are talking about here however, is the motivational gift, or in today's language, the Personality Type of the Manager. And this Personality Type is someone with a strong sense of right and wrong. In effect this Personality Type brings the gift of integrity to the table. The gift of discerning right from wrong and of speaking that into the lives of people and communities. You see this Personality Type often in social commentators and journalists. There is a very well known atheist who is both of those – a social commentator and a journalist – who lives not far from where I live. He's always in the media and whilst I disagree profoundly with some of his views, he brings a strong social conscience into the media in Australia. Integrity is very important to people with this Personality Type. Seeing things clearly, stripping away the spin, unmasking things for what they are, telling us the way things really are – that's what drives a person with the Personality Type of the Manager. They're concerned with maintaining high standards; the right standards. And they often speak for and act on behalf of the down trodden and the marginalised. You'll find them in the workplace. You'll find them in your family perhaps. And you'll find them at church. Some have strong opinions who are prepared to voice them not so much on their own. behalf, but for the purpose of bringing people to account according to what is right and what is wrong. You just want people to do the right thing and to try and do the right thing yourself to live up to that calling that's been placed on your life. In a sense, you can't help yourself – it's something that the Manager just does, because of the desire to bring people back to do the right thing.

## Brendan's Story – The Leader

These days, I'm involved in a few different things. I have a Business Coaching business, so what that means is that I talk to small business owners on how to grow their business in the areas of team building, marketing and sales. Interestingly, I am also the General Manager of a large international church. So just a quiet life really! I love accomplishment. I will do anything where you can get a result. I basically measure the success of a day, not based on how much I've done by being the leader or how much I could have done, but on what I delivered in terms of results. So I stand back and say, "That was a great day as far as I've done all these things."

The thing is, I really love taking people to new places. I love facilitating, getting results through men getting saved and built up through our men's ministry. There are quite a few other things I do too. And naturally, we have a family. God has a great sense of humour. I live with four women, my wife and three daughters. Whereas I'm this sort of Alpha Male, action man, they're really into fashion and shopping and all the great girls stuff so that's been great to round me out a little bit, but challenging at the same time.

What are the things that make me different from the other people? That's a great question. In some ways in relationships, I feel I have to really concentrate hard so that I don't have dislocated relationships. Other people would find that would be easy to them, where as I need to put structure and I need to think about that. Just finding time to spend with people. And I need to be careful that I don't squash people in terms of getting the achievement done. I have to be really careful about that. Now that I'm a little bit older, I know how to control that a bit more. When I was younger, the number of people that went away from me crying because they were just too slow or not in the process of getting it done, it was not a happy thing.

When you're this strong and this outcome focused, you can really easily overpower people. When people come up against you they really would feel that they're not in a position to fight back, whereas I would want them to fight back. But I think one of the really releasing things that I've found is that in God, I've got amazing potential and He has made me uniquely the way I am. I need to get on with my strengths but on the other side, I need to put structure and disciplines around my challenges so that I'm not too much of a loose cannon.

**Who or What Is the "Leader"?**

These days, people don't much like being told what to do. Whether it's the teenager who rolls their eyes at their parents, or the employee who deliberately undermines the authority of their manager when they disagree. There's something about where we, as a society are headed, where the notion of there being a Leader placed over the top of us, someone who barks out orders and tells us what to do, is increasingly abhorrent.

Sure, there are old styles of hierarchical leadership. And these days, there are also some more contemporary styles of inclusive and collaborative leadership. But whether it's at work, or in the home, or in a social club, or in a church – each of those groups have Leaders.

Those who lead, and those who are meant to follow their leadership. Unless you have that, you have anarchy. Have you ever tried to run anything completely by committee? It just doesn't work. So, whether or not it offends our increasingly egalitarian "I'll do whatever I like when I like" social ethic, inclination and outlook, deep down we all know that we need leadership.

So, let's come again, one last time, to this same passage in Romans Chapter 12, to locate this Personality Type of the Leader: We have gifts that differ according to the grace given to us: prophecy, in proportion to faith; ministry, in ministering; the teacher, in teaching; the exhorter, in exhortation; the giver, in generosity; the leader, in diligence; the compassionate, in cheerfulness. (Romans 12:6-8) The Leader literally is someone who is set or placed before or over us – to lead, protector, or to give help and care for and attention to those under him or her.

As I listened to Brendan telling his story too – that's what came out. A definite strength, but a strength that's under control, a strength that's being exercised for the benefit of others these days, rather than to advance his own selfish agendas and interests. And you can pick him as a Leader, because not only is he involved in a wide variety of things, not only is he competent to do those things, but in each case, he's leading and naturally, people are following. A good Leader is an enormous blessing. A bad Leader is a terrible curse. Sadly, so often in organisations, the people in leadership positions aren't made to be in those positions. They rely on rank and status, rather than on their natural gifting as a Leader. And we all find people like that difficult to follow.

**Why Is the Leader Motivated Through the Will?**

Well, the best way to describe the Leader is that in a sense, they make things happen to achieve outcomes. Any venture, anything worth doing or achieving is going to have inertia – it's going to be hard to get going. And then, it's going to face obstacles and disappointments and setbacks and confusion and delay and internal strife and the blame game and mistrust and ... it's just the way things are.

The Leader is the person who sees the objective – often by dreaming about it, sometimes for days, weeks ... even years. The best way to describe the Leader is that in a sense, they crash through things to achieve outcomes. And then, when the time is right, the Leader drives hard to achieve the outcome; to reach the goal – bringing other people with them. When the bombs are going off, and the machine guns are firing and the troops are in disarray and everyone's blaming everyone else – the Leader is the one who keeps their eyes firmly focused on the hill that they were attacking in the first place and brings everyone along to finally take that hill and seize the objective from the enemy. To do that, you have to be incredibly strong-willed. You don't do that so much by just thinking about it. You don't do that by feeling your way along through the melee, using your emotions. You don't even do that by encouraging people to achieve (although encouragement is part of leadership). You do that by sheer brute strength. By persistence. By a mighty act of will that's prepared to overcome emotions like fear and disappointment. That's why the Leader operates from the will. That's because they're in many respects quite similar. But they have an important difference.

The Achiever – a soul person – brings people along through encouragement. The Achiever wants to achieve and help other people achieve. The Leader brings people along because those people respect and trust his or her strength. They believe in their Leader and so they're prepared to follow that person into a battle. The Leader's motivation – truly, is to win. The Leader's motivation is to seize that hill. And the people whom he or she leads – it's not so much about encouraging them as about being their Leader and just knowing within yourself that it's a natural place to be and that the people who you're leading are inspired to follow you. That's the difference.

## Why Do the Rest of Us Need the Leader?

Let's go back to Brendan's story. Let's listen again to what he said: I love accomplishment. I will do anything where you can get a result. I basically measure the success of a day, not based on how much I've done or how much I could have done, but on what I achieved in terms of results. So I stand back and say, "That was a great day as far as I've achieved all these things." We are so blessed with all the different Personality Talents. Let's list them again – the Achiever, the Encourager, the Mentor, the Carer, the Giver, the Planner, the Thinker Server, the Manager and the Leader. I hope you've been as utterly gobsmacked as I've been to discover how deeply diverse and empoweringly complementary and how compellingly necessary these different members of the body are. Where would we be without any of them? Lost and incomplete is the answer. Missing part of our body – like an amputee, or a blind man, or a deaf man. But what if all these different members just headed off in their own direction? What if they just all did what naturally comes to them? Then where would we be? Well, as a crusty old sergeant in the Army once said "Sir, we'd be all over the place like a mad person's breakfast." We need someone to pull it all together. We need someone that the other people will naturally look to, to lead us to the objective. We need someone who the individual members trust enough and respect enough, to subjugate their individual needs, and individual perspectives and individual agendas, in order to achieve a common goal. Enter ... the Leader.

# PART 5

# Becoming the Person You Were Made to Be

## How do you become the person you were made to be?

The simple answer is: Be committed & join the service! It's not just a job, it's a new way of life.

By you using your gifts and talents you will fulfill your purpose. You will have an ability that others want and need when you serve others. It is God's purpose for you to serve others by using the gifts & talents you were given.

> *Therefore I urge you, brothers and sisters, by the mercies of God, to present your bodies [dedicating all of yourselves, set apart] as a living sacrifice, holy and well-pleasing to God, which is your rational (logical, intelligent) act of worship. Romans 12:1 (AMP)*

This also builds your confidence and self esteem and gives you purpose and meaning in your life through serving others with your gifts and talent. You are more attractive to others when you serve others by using your Gifts and Talents. Research shows you will be happier and healthier and live longer. There is NO selfishness in serving others, it takes away the focus on yourself. It connects you and makes new relationships by getting you involved with others and you will not be lonely. Business calls it Client or Customer Service, The Defense Force and Police call it The Service. Whether you are at work, at school, with family and friends, or wherever you are, we are serving others by using your gifts & talents to bless them.

## Use It or Lose It

In Jesus's Parable of the Talents (Mathew 25:14) the master trusts his servants to manage his goods for him while he goes away. He gives 5 talents to one, 2 talents to another and 1 talent to the other, a different measure to each one according to their ability. When the master returns the first servant who had 5 talents doubled it and had 10. The second servant who had 2 talents doubled it and had 4. The third servant who had 1 talent did not use it so the master took it from him and called him a wicked and lazy servant.

'Prices Law' says that if you take the square root of the number of your employees, say 9, 3 will do half the work and the other 6 employees will do the other half of the work. Gallup Research says that only 1 in 5 people are engaged and productive in their work. Voucher Cloud research found that the average office is only productive 3 hours a day. This is believed to be because most people do not know what their talents are and are not using them, they are in the wrong job and are productive. Try and concentrate for more than just 20 minutes to do a job or study a subject you're not suited to and you will find how hard is to do.

## Takeaways from the Parable of the Talents

1. Each of us have been given our gifts and talents but we have to go out and use them to be the person we are made to be able to fulfill our purpose. God has already given us everything we need for life and Godliness through our knowledge of Him (2 Peter 1:3)

2. God gives each of us different talents and different measures according to our ability, and trusts us to use them and He will multiply them "His grace (gifts & talents) and peace will be multiplied to us in our knowledge of God and Jesus our Lord." (2 Peter 1:2)

3. "To everyone who has, even more will be given to them and they will have abundance, but to those who do not use them, even what they have will be taken away from them." (Matthew 25:29)

4. "The master said, 'Well done, good and faithful servant! You have been faithful with a few things; I will put you in charge of many things. Come and share your master's happiness" (Matthew 25:22)

5. To the servant who didn't use his talent, he was called a wicked and lazy servant and his talent was taken from him.

**We all have our Gifts and Talents, no one misses out, but you have to know them, use and develop them to fulfill your purpose or you will lose them.**

Romans 12:2 says "... be transformed by the renewing of your mind". The word 'transformed' is a translation of the Greek word *metamorphousthe* which means to be changed from one form to another. With that in mind, let's pause and read this short story.

### The Caterpillar Story

*Dark clouds gather in the sky as my legs carry me up a flower stalk, to the leaf I had been munching on before. I sit there and munch as silent raindrops fall onto the damp soil below. I was getting bigger and bigger as I ate and that's was all I did, apart from eating, sleeping and repeating. You see that I am just a boring caterpillar who has no real purpose in life.*

*Then, out of nowhere a big beautiful butterfly with wings full of yellow and blue spots. "Jump on my back he says and I will show you your purpose" Without hesitation I jump on his back and we flew through the air, gliding through the trees and bush. "The best thing," he tells me as we pass a colony of bees, "is drinking nectar from the flowers!" I imagined myself flying high in the sky and drinking nectar from a flower. Now I knew what I wanted to become, but some how I knew it was not going to be easy. Afraid, I stumbled out onto a stick. Beady eyes looking at me from every direction, wondering if I was going to fall. But I am going to commit 100% to fulfilling my purpose by spending 8 days in a cocoon, alone and not eating, to become the butterfly that I was made to be.*

*Knees knocking, I took my place on the stick and soon I was engulfed in darkness by my own chrysalis. The loneliness and despair surrounded me. "When was this going to end" I say as I fall into another deep sleep. I wake up to a beam of light shining through a gap in my chrysalis. The sun warms my face as I breath-in the fresh new air. I lift off and am soaring above the canopy with the birds and diving down to streams with the fish. I land on a wild-flower and drink the sweet, juicy nectar. it's incredible. I am amazed that I get to live this amazing life, for this is my purpose.*

- By Olivia Moran

## Caterpillar or Butterfly?

This is a beautiful story of transformation and purpose. The caterpillar felt like it had no purpose in life, but through a chance encounter with a beautiful butterfly, it discovered its true calling. It took courage and commitment for the caterpillar to transform itself into a butterfly, but it was willing to do whatever it took to fulfil its purpose.

This story teaches us that sometimes we may feel like we have no purpose or direction in life, but if we keep our eyes and hearts open, we may find our true calling. It may take effort and sacrifice, but the rewards can be incredible.
It is also a reminder that transformation and growth can be difficult and uncomfortable, but it is necessary for us to reach

our full potential. We may experience moments of loneliness and despair, but if we stay focused on our goal, we can emerge from the darkness stronger and more beautiful than ever before. By using our commitment to learn, understand and going out and doing it, we will find our purpose in life In the end, the caterpillar discovered that its purpose was to become a butterfly and experience the beauty of life. We too can discover our purpose and find joy and fulfilment in our lives. All it takes is the courage to take a leap of faith and commit ourselves to our purpose.

Let's use God's Personality System to look at a Caterpillar:

| Function | It eats up to 3 times its body weight every day on leaves and can cause extensive damage to fruit trees, crops and plants |
|---|---|
| Purpose | To transform into a butterfly |
| Talent | To be able to fly |
| Identity | To be a butterfly |
| Attraction | Its beautiful wings |
| Butterfly's PURPOSE | To pollinate the flowers |

The caterpillar did not come into the world to be a caterpillar. It has a higher purpose, a higher calling to be transformed into a beautiful butterfly.

**This is the perfect will of God for your life**

*"Do not conform to the pattern of this world, but be transformed by the renewing of your mind. Then you will be able to test and approve what God's will is—his good, pleasing and perfect will."*
*Romans 12:2 (NIV)*

Do not conform - you were not born to just be in the world but be tranformed, you were born to be the person you were made to be, so that you can fulfill your potential and your purpose.

**How do you transform?**

- By knowing your gifts and talents
- By renewing your mind, by learning how wonderfully you are made.
- By going out and proving for yourself what the perfect will of God for your life is.
- Your purpose is to grow and multiply your gifts and talents, so that you can become the amazing person you were made to be; so that you can lead a fulfilled joyful and purposeful life.

*"For I say through the grace (God's gifts & favour) given to me and to everyone of you, do not think of yourself more highly than you ought to think..." Romans 12:3*

**Why is God giving us this warning?**

The Passion translation of the same verse (Romans 12:3): *"God has given me grace to speak a warning about pride. I would ask each of you to be emptied of self-promotion and not create a false image of your own importance."*

So why this warning? Because pride is one of the deadly sins that leads to failure. It is God who has given each of us our Gifts so we should always think of them "soberly as God has given a measure to each one of us, of trust".

# PART 6

# More Amazing
# Things
# About You

**"It's not how smart you are... it's where you are smart"**

You wouldn't expect a tradesperson to use the wrong tools as they would do a bad job. So why would you employ a person with the wrong intelligence (the wrong tools) and expect them to do a good job?

Howard Gardner, a professor at Harvard University, developed the theory of Multiple Intelligence in the early 1980s. He documented 9 or more intelligences where each person is more dominant in one intelligence, making them more productive for a particular type of task and work. Research has found that if a person's work is aligned with their intelligence, they are much more likely to be happier, healthier and up to three times more productive than someone whose intelligence is not aligned with their work.

Dr. Win Wenger, a doctor and author who looks at brain function said "that unless we fully understand how our brains work, and how they relate to intelligence, we may never even approach proper functioning. Within all of us is the potential for genius. It is there for us to know, develop, explore and enjoy."

**Why do 47% of millennials wish they had chosen a different career?**

As millennials began to turn 40 in 2021, CNBC launched *Middle-Aged Millennials*, a series exploring how the oldest members of this generation have grown into adulthood amidst the backdrop of the Great Recession and the Covid-19 pandemic, student loans, stagnant wages and rising costs of living.

Alfenito works as a cashier at a bakery in Morgantown, West Virginia US. Thinking back to her college days, "I wish someone had helped me figure out what jobs would be applicable for my interests and passions, and what kind of degree was actually required for that — if any," Alfenito says.

Many older millennials who are now approaching middle age have significant career regrets. Nearly half, 47%, say they wish they had chosen a different career path when they started out, according to a recent survey of 1,000 U.S. adults ages 33 to 40, conducted by The Harris Poll on behalf of CNBC. Alfenito believes millennials, who range in age from 25 to 40 and make up the largest age group in the workforce, were pressured to pursue four-year degrees, and the mountains of debt that can come with them, without always knowing if there was a viable career on the other side of graduation. As older millennials approach two decades in the workforce, their current roles and responsibilities may not be what they envisioned out of high school or college and what they would do differently if they could start over again.

So that you don't also fall into the trap of choosing the wrong career, make sure you understand God's Personality System and other information to make an informed decision on your natural gifts and talents. Also talk with people in the occupations that interest you, especially people who love what they are doing and are good at it.

In the following pages we will look in more detail at subject choices, career options, learning preferences, relationship style and ministries that are best suited to your personality.

## Your Learning Preferences

Where possible try and use your learning preference in school, business, your own environment, small groups, etc as you will learn better this way. Recent research shows that our learning style preferences tend to prefer a style that suits your gifts, talents and your intelligence.

READING/WRITING/MATHS
*A more logical, facts based preference*
- Formal classroom teaching
- Reading/studying
- Talking/presenting
- Maths/problem solving
- Projects

VISUALISING
*A more flexible, holistic, options preference*
- Exploring possibilities
- Creative options
- Designs & concepts
- Graphs & charts
- Brainstorming

TACTILE
*A more linear, sequential preference*
- Hands-on activities
- Practical examples
- Researching details
- Planning projects
- Clear structured steps

AUDITORY
*An expressive, feeling, experiential preference*
- Interacting with others
- Sharing experiences
- Informal, relaxed settings
- Experiential learning
- Artistic opportunities

## Your Subject Preferences

Try to study the subjects that would best fit your talents and that could best suits your career options and what interests you most, then talk with people in the industry to get more information.

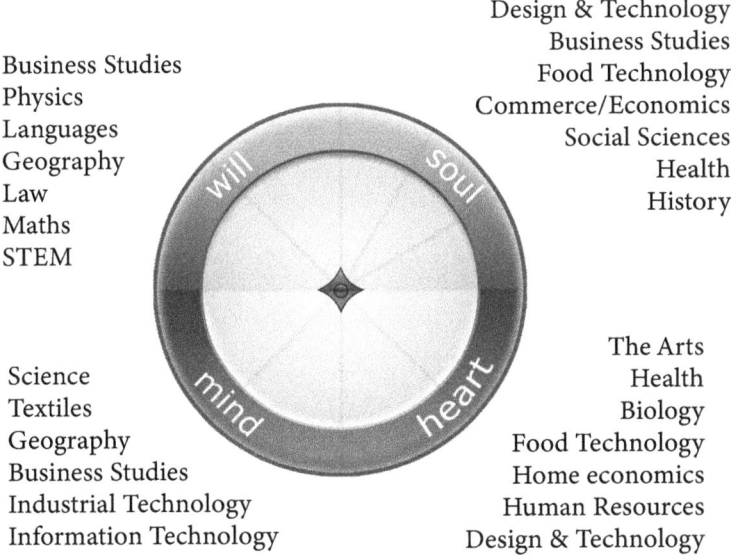

Business Studies
Physics
Languages
Geography
Law
Maths
STEM

Design & Technology
Business Studies
Food Technology
Commerce/Economics
Social Sciences
Health
History

Science
Textiles
Geography
Business Studies
Industrial Technology
Information Technology

The Arts
Health
Biology
Food Technology
Home economics
Human Resources
Design & Technology

## Career Options for you

You know how important it is to find a career that you would be good at doing, but where do you start? There are many jobs that would suit you, so look at what careers fall into your talents and what interests you, then talk with people in the industry to get more information. Start here:

Lawyer, Finance, Sales, Military, Real Estate Agent, Journalist, CEO, Project Leader, Police, Finance, Surgeon, Engineer, Business Manager, Project

Architect, Pilot, CEO, Marketing, Sales, Entrepeneur, Designer, Surgeon, Town Planner, Landscaper, Consultant

Manager, Teacher, Accountant, Engineer, Finance, Legal, Administrator, Ai, Robotics, Consultant, Advisor, Logistics

Sales, Marketing, Teacher, Trainer, Advertising Entrepeneur, Journalist, Landscaper, Physiotherapist

Software, Research, Analyst, Pathologist, AI, Robotics, Statistician, Actuary, Scientist, Environmentalist

Teacher, Trainer, Counsellor, Client Service, HR, Psychologist, PA

Kindergarten Teacher, Doctor, Nurse, Carer, Graphic/Interior/Fashion Designer, Artist, Social Media, Writer, Ambulance

Trades Person, Police, Military, Nurse, Geologist, Administration, Accountant Bookkeeper, Drone Pilot, Marketing, Technology, IT, Medical Technician

Customer Service, Healthcare, Retail, Physiotherapist, Teacher, Social Worker, HR, Cook/Chef, Counsellor, Office Positions

*will, soul, mind, heart*

# Your Attraction & Relationship Style

**Self-Controlled** – to relate with people in a decisive, helpful and disciplined wa.y

**Patience** – to be active but with perseverance while being patient.

**Goodness** – to be virtuous, morally upright trustworthy and good.

**Joyful** – a state of joyful happiness in all situations.

**Peaceful** – being calm supportive, agreeable, and receptive to people

**Gentleness** – a quiet understanding with helpful wisdom.

**Caring** – self giving in love and compassion and caring for others.

**Faithfulness** – a trustworthy, reliable friend who does what they say they will do.

**Kind** – kindness shown through giving and helping people.

## Match your ministries to your personality

Start with an easy ministry such as welcoming people in your church, school, or work. Then work out where you could best use your talents, and offer yourself for the position, should it be available. Once you start moving in your gifts you will see many more opportunities arrive for you.

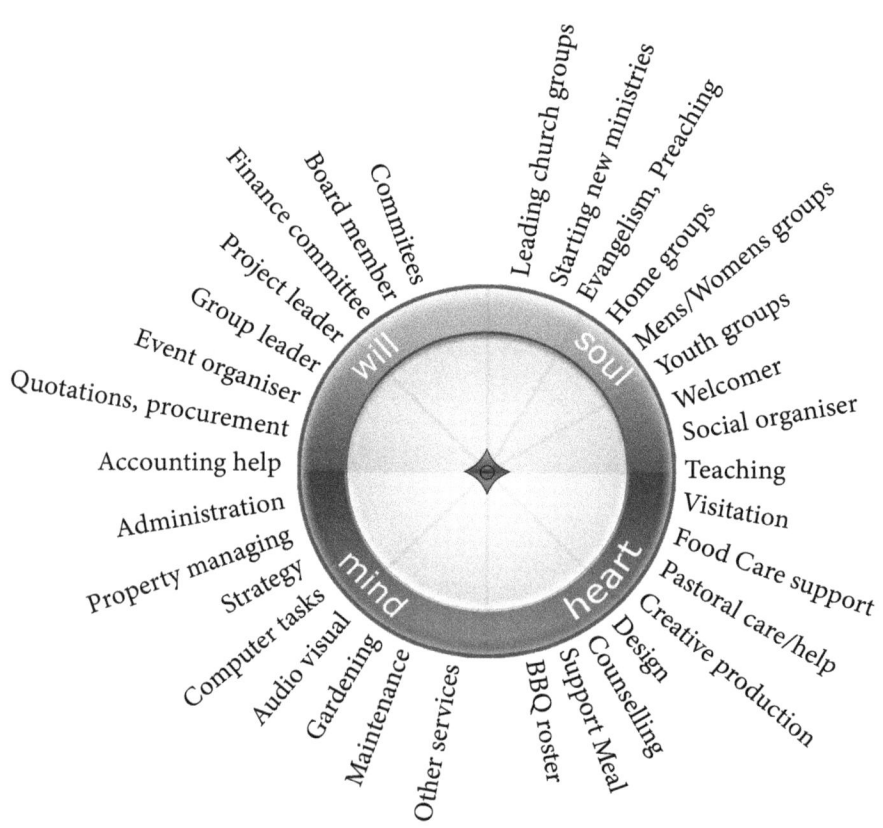

Now we have come to the end of discovering God's Personality System, you might want to fill in your own Profile here:

Subjective or Objective Thinking? (page 33)

_____

Main personality (pages 34-37)

_____

Secondary personality (page 38)

_____

Main talent (pages 64-77)

_____

Secondary talent (page 78)

_____

Learning preferences (page 130)

_____

Subject preferences (page 131)

_____

Career options (page 132)

_____

Ministries (page 134)

_____

## What do people say about 'GPS'

*"What an incredible tragedy it would be to get to the end of your life, only to look back and realise that you've wasted it. We only get one crack at this life – there are no dress rehearsals, so it's profoundly important that we discover who we are. My good friend Keith Henry has dedicated his life to helping men, women and students, young and old – to unpack God's Word to discover their purpose, gifts and abilities.*
*God's Personality System is a powerful tool that provides a clear presentation of the bible truth that each one of us is made to function differently. You will be able to locate your best direction in life, how you function, your purpose, your gifts and talents, your personality and your identity."*
**Berni Dymet Bible teacher/CEO ChristianityWorks**

*"I see many patients on a daily basis, who suffer from many stress related conditions. Many of these conditions and their causes relate back to not knowing our identity or purpose, we then suffer from a lack of confidence and struggle in decision making and life generally."*
**Mike Hubbard Doctor of Osteopathic Medicine**

*"Having used GPS for several years with my business clients, and organisations that I have managed, GPS has proven time and time again to be a very practical way to identify people's natural talents. It helps me quickly pin-point where people are*

*naturally gifted and talented, to find their best fit into their roles and their careers to be able to better fulfil their purpose. I have found the GPS instrument, developed by Keith Henry, to be incredibly accurate and easy to use"*

**Leo Krikman, Director of Business Consulting and Performance Coaching**

Printed in the USA
CPSIA information can be obtained
at www.ICGtesting.com
LVHW072103101124
796067LV00019B/340